People of the Way

*Pray Now Devotions, Reflections,
Blessings and Prayer Activities*

Published on behalf of
THE PRAY NOW GROUP

SAINT ANDREW PRESS
Edinburgh

First published in 2016 by Saint Andrew Press
SAINT ANDREW PRESS
121 George Street
Edinburgh EH2 4YN

978 0 86153 992 5

Please note that the views expressed in 'Pray Now' are those of the
individual writer and not necessarily the official view of the Church of
Scotland, which can be laid down only by the General Assembly.

British Library Cataloguing in Publication Data
A catalogue record for this book is available from the British Library.

It is the publisher's policy to only use papers that are natural and
recyclable and that have been manufactured from timber grown in
renewable, properly managed forests. All of the manufacturing processes
of the papers are expected to conform to the environmental regulations of
the country of origin.

Typeset in Times by Waverley Typesetters, Norfolk
Printed and bound in the United Kingdom by CPI Group (UK) Ltd

Contents

Preface   vi

Using this Book   vii

The Way

1	Seeking	2
2	Uncharted Territory	4
3	Burden	6
4	Detours	8
5	Passing Places	10
6	Crossroads	12
7	Wayside	14
8	Desert	16
9	Signposts	20
10	Discovery	24

The Way Within

11	Prayer	28
12	Meditation	30
13	Identity	32
14	Incarnation	34
15	Gender	36
16	Forgiveness	40
17	Grace	44
18	Stillness	46
19	Lament	50
20	Disciplined	54
21	Resistance	56
22	Vulnerability	58
23	Dependent/Independent	60

24	Exile	62
25	Poor in Spirit	66
26	Sacrificial	70

The Way Among

27	Worship	74
28	Gathered	76
29	Welcome	80
30	Inclusion	84
31	Queer	86
32	Holding Things in Common	90
33	Learning Together	94
34	Nurturing	96
35	Prophetic	98
36	Dispersed	102
37	Persecuted	104
38	Ritual	108
39	Rites of Passage	110
40	Random	114
41	Companionship	118
42	Common Memory	122

The Way Beyond

43	Beyond the Pale	126
44	Now and Not Yet	128
45	Beyond the Horizon	132
46	Otherness of God	134
47	Over the Edge	138
48	Letting Go	140
49	Dying	142
50	Resurrection	146
51	Heaven	150
52	Revelation	154

Prayer Activities

Prayer Activity 1	Seeking Refuge	158
Prayer Activity 2	Being Tested	162
Prayer Activity 3	Sacrificing	166

Prayer Activity 4	Resurrecting	170
Prayer Activity 5	Living in the Spirit	174
Prayer Activity 6	Forgiving	178
Prayer Activity 7	Resting	182
Prayer Activity 8	Expressing	186
Prayer Activity 9	Learning	190
Prayer Activity 10	Harvesting	194
Prayer Activity 11	Waiting	198
Prayer Activity 12	Incarnating	202

Acknowledgements   206

Preface

'Follow me,' said Jesus. This is our invitation to be people of the way and journey with Christ through the heights and depths of human experience. Those who have travelled the way before us found their journey was marked by encounters with God. The characters we read about in the Bible and the hymns and songs we sing in worship, speak to us of a God who travels with us along the way.

'Pray Now: People of the Way' is a valuable book to take with us on the journey. As I read I found myself wrestling with some of the themes and concepts and although not always comfortable, appreciated being challenged. This collection of Scripture Readings, Meditations and Prayers is a rich treasure store. With sensitivity and depth, the 52 reflections lead us to meet with God in the situations and relationships of life, as well as in our hopes and fears for the future. Where work is done, meals are shared, news is received, tears are shed or laughter is shared, keep this book close to hand so that its words may nurture encounters with God.

REVD DAN CARMICHAEL
Vice-Convener, Resourcing Worship

Using this Book

Jesus said to him, 'I am the way, and the truth and the life.
No one comes to the Father except through me.'

~ John 14:6 ~

'People of the Way' is the theme of this edition of 'Pray Now' and is a prayer resource for people across all denominations and none. 'People of the Way' echoes the Church of Scotland's theme for their 'Heart and Soul' year of celebration 2016–17.

Jesus described himself as 'the way'. The writers have explored 'the way': firstly as a faith and lifestyle model as taught and lived out by Jesus; secondly as the means by which we are put right with God through Jesus' death on the Cross.

The contents of the book invite you to explore what it means to be a 'person of the way' and part of a 'people of the way' through prayer, reflection and activity. Hopefully, 'Pray Now: People of the Way' will be able to engage, encourage, challenge and comfort you wherever you are 'on the way' in your present life.

We have divided the book into four sections. The first is simply called 'The Way' and is about journey and pilgrimage. Each title reflects a moment of travelling or encounter or discerning or deciding along the way.

The second section is 'The Way Within' and focuses on our inner journey and transformation. Each title reflects a spiritual quality or a mind-set that is of the essence of being a child of God, a follower of Christ and a channel for the gifts of the Holy Spirit.

The third section is 'The Way Among' and looks at the vertical and horizontal relationships of the community of faith: how we relate to God, to each other and to the wider community. Each title identifies a characteristic or practice of people who are gathered by the Spirit to be the body of Christ in a particular place – worshipping, witnessing, working and learning together while sharing the joys and sorrows of everyday life.

The final section is 'The Way Beyond' and contemplates that which is beyond our present knowledge, understanding and experience. Each title invites reflection on the transcendent God who is present to us in Christ and the Holy Spirit but whom we 'know only in part' but one day hope to see face to face and know fully. For now, we are 'a people of faith' who trust in God's promises.

The former chief rabbi, Dr Jonathan Sacks, wrote,

> *'Like music, prayer is a natural expression of human longing,*
> *evidence of the image of God within us all.'*

Everyone needs to pray and everyone can pray. Prayer can involve using silence, listening, speaking or completing an action. Prayer can be guided or spontaneous. Prayer may be individual, shared with friend or family, or part of a communal act of worship.

The format of 'Pray Now' is to have 52 chapters, allowing the book to be used both as a weekly and a daily resource for prayer.

Each chapter offers the following:

- a Biblical verse that has stimulated the content for the week (taken from the New Revised Standard Version unless otherwise stated)
- a short meditation
- a morning prayer
- an evening prayer
- two suggestions for Scriptural reading
- a blessing.

Some users may wish to use one chapter for seven days, while others may wish to dip in and out of the content over the week, perhaps supplemented by some of the additional prayer activities.

There are 12 Prayer Activities, which variously invite observation, self-awareness, self-appraisal, reflection, thanksgiving and praying for others. They invite you to explore your journey of faith, discipleship and mission. All activities can be used for individual devotion but some are very apt for group activity.

Each Prayer Activity page may form a prayer project for a few weeks, as the prayer activities both echo and also extend some of the titles in the 52 chapters. All activities lead with a classical or modern quotation and include blank pages for your notes: thoughts that occur to you, a reminder, a form of diary or a quotation from the Bible or another source – maybe even something somebody said to you that day. Also, you could invite someone else to write something for you. This ensures that your copy of 'Pray Now' will become unique!

'Pray Now' may be used for individual devotions, prayer groups or as a resource for reflective worship events.

However you choose to use 'Pray Now', the writers pray that your interaction with the book will provide encouragement and inspiration in your prayer life. We may not have all the right words for where you are at the moment, and there will always be times when words are not enough, but remember, as John Bunyan said:

'In prayer it is better to have a heart without words than words without a heart.'

REVD CAROL FORD
Convener of Pray Now *Writers Group*

For more information, the guide '*How to Pray*' can be found on the Church of Scotland website at www.churchofscotland. org.uk/worship or phone 0131 225 5722 and ask to be put through to the Mission and Discipleship Council.

THE WAY

*The places, the events and the signs
on our journey towards God.*

*Jesus went on with his disciples to the villages of Caesarea
    Philippi;
and on the way he asked his disciples 'Who do you say that I am?'*

~ Mark 8:27 ~

Seeking

Ask and it will be given to you;
seek and you will find;
knock and the door will be opened to you.

~ Matthew 7:7 ~

Meditation

Sometimes, I have to squint to make You out,
stretch up to see over the crowd,
push past the busyness and noise.

Sometimes, I just shut my eyes,
and there You are,
not hiding,
just waiting.

The unknown of each moment,
the possibility that I can't quite grasp,
the spaces in between.

I think that's where You live,
not hiding,
just waiting,
waiting to be found.

Morning Prayer

I awaken in Your presence Lord.
You are to be found here.
Help me to recognise You
in my coming and my going,
in my searching and my finding.
Guide me, so I may step boldly forward in faith
and find all that You want me to discover today.
Go beyond and behind,
to my left and my right,
that whatever way I seek to go,
I will surely find You in everything
and everyone I meet.   AMEN

Evening Prayer

In the decisions made, right or wrong,
in the words now said that cannot be unsaid,
in all my fears, failures and shortcomings,
thank You for the gift of Your presence.

To see You in the familiar,
to recognise You in the not yet,
in the midst of all that I hope and dream for,
may I seek You O God,
and find You in the day to come.   AMEN

Scripture Readings

Matthew 7:7–12   *Seek and you will find*
Matthew 6:25–34   *Seek the Kingdom of God above
all else*

Blessing

Lord of all knowing,
grant me eyes to see,
grant me ears to hear,
grant me truth to find
and courage to seek.   AMEN

Uncharted Territory

Your word is a lamp to my feet and a light to my path.

~ Psalm 119:105 ~

Meditation

As you journey through life
you meet obstacles along the way.
As you choose the paths to follow
you find yourself walking through vast open spaces,
through bright sunlit vistas,
sometimes green pastures
and sometimes deserts.

But, occasionally the path is not so clear,
not so easy to walk.
Perhaps it seems too small to fit yourself down,
like you have to squeeze in
and shimmy along at a slower, more laboured pace.
While you may long, even pray,
for your circumstances to change
and this path to widen
so that you can breathe easy once more,
you sometimes miss the subtlety of our situation.

It may be, in this hardship,
that we find the greatest of answers
to the smallest of questions.

Morning Prayer

As the stars in the night sky
guide travellers, sailors,
even kings,
I pray that Your light, O Lord,
would guide me.
As the morning star
heralds the dawning of a new day,
I set off on another journey.
Show me where to make anchor
in safe harbours

or to avoid the rocks of temptation
that would throw me off course.
Set my compass
that I may always point to You.   AMEN

Evening Prayer

Tired from the journey,
a weary soul
worn down by the weight of the world.
Help me to shake off the dust
of this unfamiliar land
and rest easy
knowing You, God,
are my constant companion
on my travels.   AMEN

Scripture Readings

Psalm 119	*Your word is a lamp to my feet and a light to my path.*
Proverbs 3:5–6	*Trust in the Lord with all your heart*

Blessing

May the blessing of light be upon you,
within you
and around you.

May the blessing of light shine out from you,
like the welcoming glow of the house on the horizon,
bidding the wanderer –
'*Come in and find shelter*'.   AMEN

Burden

If I make my bed in Sheol, you are there.

~ Psalm 139:8b ~

Meditation

It's a cold February night.
I gently ease the car out of the frosty driveway.
'We'll just go for a drive; it's a nice night for it.'

And yet,
I know it's not.
The drive will end with a painful kiss goodbye,
that sees her
left behind on the other side of the swing doors.

The ward
will be a place of security and safety
until she reaches an equilibrium again
and finds peace in the confusion
of her illness.

Her memory of this night will distort
and she will struggle to see
that I did this out of love
and I will always be here for her.

Others have left.
Friends, lovers, family,
fearful of what might happen.
Tears and exhaustion
become too much.

They cruelly label her
as a burden.

I couldn't.
She's loved.
I'm loved
by God.

And that's just enough
to keep us both going
on a cold February night.

Morning Prayer

Break into this loneliness, God.
Confront my confusion.
Help me to know who I am
and who I am called to be.
Lift me up on eagles' wings.
Let me run and not be weary.
Give me courage to leave behind
a world of labels and limitations
until the dawn of all that is possible
comes to me.   AMEN

Evening Prayer

As I rest, cast Your love on those who are restless;
bless those who are lost in mental illness.
Encourage those who love beyond stigma
and help us all to understand and love more
until Your Kingdom comes.   AMEN

Scripture Readings

Psalm 139	*Lord you search me and you know me*
1 Corinthians 12:22–26	*Strength in community and understanding of one another*

Blessing

May the God of strength move within you.
May the God of courage hear your distress.
May the God of hope reveal wholeness to you.
May the God of the dawn defeat your darkness.

Detours

When Pharaoh let the people go, God did not lead them by way of the land of the Philistines, although that was nearer ...

[Instead] God led the people by the roundabout way of the wilderness towards the Red Sea.

~ Exodus 13:17–18 ~

Meditation

In the rush to get
from A to B
from one chore to the next
from the reality of today to the dreams of tomorrow
small inconveniences get in the way.

Every second not going forward
is a second lost.
Every step to the side
is a moment wasted.
Each detour lies in ambush
to rob us of our precious cargo.
Every diversion steals a vital opportunity
from our desire to obtain, and achieve, and amass
all that we can.

But what good is it to gain the whole world,
if we lose our own soul?
For in every detour
is the chance to explore new ways
and each diversion gives us
an opportunity to see things from a different perspective.

So, take time to meander with God;
to escape the fast lane
and explore the waysides of life.
Learn from the detours
and find the rambling route of God.

Morning Prayer

Assist me, God, in living hopefully into the future.
As traditional signposts are swept away

and the way ahead seems unsure
help me to set my worries aside
as I tread new routes.

Guide my footsteps
and lead me away from the fast lane of life,
that rushes towards oblivion.
Open my eyes to the possibilities
not seen from the main route.
Open my ears to the news
not heard among the clamour for success.   AMEN

Evening Prayer

Loving God,
in an out-of-the-way place,
where few folk ever visited,
You came in all Your glory.

Help me to tread out of the way
and lead me to
the places
the people
and the opportunities
that reveal Your glory today.   AMEN

Scripture Readings

Exodus 13:17–18   *A detour in the wilderness*
Matthew 2:12   *The Magi take an alternative route home*

Blessing

Bless, O God,
each step I take on the journey of life,
that I may tread with care, courage, and hope.   AMEN

Passing Places

And he said to them,
'What are you discussing with each other while you walk along?'
They stood still, looking sad.

~ Luke 24:17 ~

Meditation

Eyes downcast on the morning commute,
we rarely look into the faces of those with whom we travel.
All have their own story
their own share of burdens and joys.
But, for this moment, our journeys collide
and there is opportunity
to share a smile,
a word of greeting or acknowledgement.
In that early morning light
vulnerability is present,
unmasked by the dawn,
laid bare to the prospect
of a new day.
In those moments
and places of passing,
spirit calls to spirit
and there is shared purpose,
a mutuality
in which we can accommodate the other
and, in that accommodation,
find our own needs met.

Morning Prayer

God, who journeys with us
in every moment of the day,
in this morning light
awaken us to Your light
in the eyes of those
with whom we share our journey.
As we step aside to let others pass
or as we merge into the throng,
give to us an awareness

of shared anxieties and blessings
and a willingness
to accommodate the other.
Throughout this day
as we are drawn into
the passing places of life
may we know our needs met
in making way for others
and may we sense Your presence
in every space we inhabit.   AMEN

Evening Prayer

God, You met us in the light of dawn
and journeyed with us through the day.
We glimpsed You in our travels:
in our fellow commuters,
in the newspaper vendor,
in the weary ticket collector,
and in the boisterous child
who cheered our journey home.
We give You thanks for all those passing places
we experienced today,
those places where others made way for us
and where we were enabled to make way for others.
As our day ends, we bring to You all those
whom we met on the way today,
known to You by name,
beloved children of God;
and we commit them, along with ourselves,
into Your care this night.   AMEN

Scripture Readings

Psalm 42:4–8   *Deep calls to deep*
Luke 24:15–35   *Meeting Jesus on the way*

Blessing

May the blessing of God
who inhabits every space
and accompanies us on every journey
guard and keep us
in every passing place of life.   AMEN

Crossroads

The Gifts of Wisdom
Does not wisdom call,
and does not understanding raise her voice?
On the heights, beside the way,
at the crossroads she takes her stand.

~ Proverbs 8:1–2 ~

Meditation

The Crossroads:
A place where roads meet
and pilgrims gather,
where cultures become entwined
and lines are blurred.
A place of decisions –
this way or that,
now or later,
with company or in solitude?
A place of possibility
that summons potential.
A place of promise
that seeks fulfilment.
A place of dread or expectations
where choices are made
that affect the rest of the journey
for good or ill.
A place where the Spirit of God meets us
and beckons us on
in the journey.

Morning Prayer

At every crossroad we encounter today, O God,
may we know You directing our path,
calling out to us the road we should take.
In every decision that confronts us,
may we know Your Spirit at large,
guiding our discernment,
affirming our choices,

nudging us to be confident
in Your illuminating presence,
and may we be assured
that the paths You call us to travel
lead to life in all its fullness.   AMEN

Evening Prayer

As we reflect on this day, O God,
may we see clearly all the ways You directed us
in Your path of life.
We give thanks for Your guidance,
for taking away our fear of getting it wrong,
for giving us the confidence to follow You
even when the journey is long
and the destination is uncertain.
We thank You for all those we encountered on our way.
May we have left them with a glimpse of Your love
and shared with them a measure of Your grace;
and may we too be enriched by encountering You
present in every friend and stranger.
May the rest that we now take
strengthen and enable us
for the rest of the journey with You.   AMEN

Scripture Readings

     Proverbs 8:1–11   *Where Wisdom is found*
     Matthew 7:12–17   *The narrow way*

Blessing

     God's blessing be on our journey;
     Christ's calling direct our paths;
     and the Spirit's energy lighten our step
     until we find our way home.   AMEN

Wayside

When anyone hears the word of the kingdom and does not understand it, the evil one comes and snatches away what is sown in the heart; this is what was sown on the path.

~ Matthew 13:19 ~

Meditation

Every day people trip and tumble –
in hospital wards,
on street corners,
in offices,
and family homes;
and we pass by.

Every day, people cry out for help –
in classrooms,
waiting rooms,
hotel rooms,
and boardrooms;
and we pass by.

Every day, people fall by the wayside of life.
They need someone to pick them up;
they need someone to give them help;
they need someone to set them on their feet again.
And those people are us.

For, whenever we pass by,
we are the ones who have fallen by the wayside of faith;
we are the ones who have stumbled as disciples;
we are the ones whose souls need to be healed.

Morning Prayer

Gracious God,
You have given us eyes –
but all too often we fail to see the hurts of others.
You have given us ears –
but all too often we fail to hear the needs of others.
You have given us hearts –
but all too often we fail to love others.

Forgive us,
that our egos are bigger than our hearts;
that our praise is stifled by our criticism;
that our charity is overshadowed by our greed
and that our love is hidden by our apathy.

Help us to experience the world
and others
as You do
that we may respond in the ways
You know we can.   AMEN

Evening Prayer

Lord God of Love,
You have planted Your words
of Faith, Hope, Peace, and Justice
within my soul.
And You provide me
with the opportunities
to practise and grow them.

Help me to tend and nourish
these tender seedlings of life
and grow them into
strong trunks of faith
able to support me in Your service.   AMEN

Scripture Readings

Matthew 13:1–9 and 18–23   *The Parable of the Sower*
Luke 10:25–37   *The Parable of the Good Samaritan*

Blessing

May the blessing of God enfold you,
may God's love light all your way,
may the grace of Christ guide your footsteps
and the Spirit empower you each day.   AMEN

Desert

I am about to do a new thing;
now it springs forth, do you not perceive it?
I will make a way in the wilderness and rivers in the desert.

~ Isaiah 43:19 ~

Meditation

We overcome our obstacles
like streams running through the land,
rushing round mountains,
eroding barriers,
washing away the debris
forever flowing.

Then, we meet the desert –
the barrier that we cannot cross,
where endless sands consume our water
and our old ways no longer wash.
We find ourselves stuck,
caught in the quagmire.

But to pass this place,
we must remain in it –
long enough to let go of our old ways,
long enough to lose ourselves,
long enough to hear the voice
calling us to surrender.

As the water surrenders to the heat of the desert
becoming a raincloud,
so, too we surrender,
to rise in re-creation,
becoming something entirely new,
not just flowing on the land,
but flying on the wind,
not just crossing the desert,
but showering fresh water on it,
not just reaching the place beyond,
but blessing it

with the waters of life,
and the wisdom of the desert.

~ Adapted from a traditional wisdom meditation ~

Morning Prayer

This day, Lord,
if I rush to the top of the mountains,
help me stop
and take time,
to greet You in the foothills.

If I am eager to plunge into the sea,
help me stop
and take time,
to see You at the water's edge.

And if I try to hurry through the desert,
help me stop
and take time – however long that time takes –
to remain there,
while my soul learns to hear the voice,
of the One
who is making all things new.   AMEN

Evening Prayer

When our thirst has led us
to seek streams of living water ...
thank You, God.

When our failing strength has taught us
to lay down what we need not carry ...
thank You, God.

When the heat of the sun has forced us
to find protection and shelter in You ...
thank You, God.

Where our loneliness has drawn us
to discover our soul's true life and love in You ...
thank You, God.

Scripture Readings

Matthew 4:1–11   *The temptation of Jesus*
Exodus 17:1–7   *Water from the rock*

Blessing

Ba-ruch a-tah a-do-nai, e-lo-hei-nu me-lech ha-o-lam,
ha-go-mel le-cha-ya-vim to-vot,
sheg-mo-la-ni tov.

Blessed are You, Lord our God, King of the Universe,
who bestows kindness even to the undeserving,
and thus You have also been gracious with me.

Omein. Mi she-g'mol-chah tov hu yigmol-chah kol tov
selah.

AMEN. May He who bestowed goodness upon you, bestow
upon you all good.

~ *Jewish blessing said for someone who had returned from the desert* ~

PRAYER NOTES

Signposts

Thus says the LORD:
Stand at the crossroads, and look,
*   and ask for the ancient paths,*
where the good way lies; and walk in it,
*   and find rest for your souls.*

~ Jeremiah 6:16 ~

Meditation

It's easy to get lost in the wild places,
the exciting places,
the places of peril and risk.
Mountains are high there,
and valleys sheer and steep.
Rivers form barriers,
flowing slowly, majestically,
their depth full of menacing life.
Streams run fast, over ancient boulders,
sometimes meeting a precipice
and falling into whirlpools
far below,
stirring up the waters
into cauldrons of fear.

Such places have no easy roads,
no walkways where feet find hold,
no bridges for crossing
an alarming abyss.

But there are trails,
walked on by others,
some in the long forgotten past,
some as recent as yesterday.

Those walkers left signposts,
markers by which
the ancient path can be found,
the good way,
the way that leads to life –
and to rest for the soul.

Morning Prayer

Lord God,
I'm excited as I open my eyes
and I wonder what this day may hold,
for me, for my household,
for my friends,
for the world.
New things will happen;
there will be obstacles to overcome,
new pathways to navigate:
no two days are ever the same.
But I'm excited, Lord,
for You have marked the way I should go
with love;
You have set signposts
at all the crossroads of life,
and You have handed me a map
by which to determine
the goal of the journey.
And, best of all,
You walk with me,
sharing the journey,
teaching, upholding
and blessing me,
every step of the way
home to You.
Thank You, Lord,
in Jesus' name.   AMEN

Evening Prayer

Yes, Lord, it's been a good day,
a full day,
a day that kept me going
from morning to now.
Thank You for the day
and for the people who shared it with me.
Thank You for those who crossed my path,
and exchanged a greeting or a smile.
Thank You for those who walked with me for a while,

who told me their story and listened to mine.
Thank You for those who were there
in my need,
and for those who needed me.
And thank You for those who pointed me
in the right direction,
who showed me the way I should go.
Bless them, Lord, this night,
and give them rest,
and an exciting new day.
In Jesus' name.   AMEN

Scripture Readings

Deuteronomy 10   *The law and its essence*
John 1   *One points to the Messiah*

Blessing

May you honour the Lord your God
and walk in His way.
May you serve the Lord your God
with all your heart and with all your soul.
May you love the Lord your God
today, tomorrow, and for ever.   AMEN

PRAYER NOTES

Discovery

For with much wisdom comes much sorrow;
the more knowledge, the more grief.

~ Ecclesiastes 1:18 ~

Meditation

1543, the sun did not orbit the earth.
Copernicus published his discovery.
Some deny it for years.

1859, Darwin theorised on evolution.
Nothing is ever fully realised.
Some think their beliefs
are the exception.

1927, Lemaitre began the universe
with a tiny dot and big bang.
Some insist on a literal Genesis:
two contradictory creation stories.

1983, Montagnier and Gallo proved
the existence of HIV and opened
avenues toward a cure.
Some declare it
God's punishment for gays.

Let's try to understand:
it is hard when things that
have been known are now known
to be wrong,
when gains of knowledge
bring loss and grief
for what once felt certain.

Wisdom is accompanied by
its playmate, Sorrow.
Every new solid ground
turns old solids into liquid.

When we journey
the landscape changes

and we try to keep track.
You do not change,
but what we'd see
and understand
with Your eyes
is always in flux.

Morning Prayer

I thought I'd seen it all!
After years of careful attention,
after the month I've had,
after yesterday's astonishments,
there can be nothing new under the sun

except everything I've misremembered,
the shattering of prejudice,
the wisdom You set within outstretched reach.

Forgive me when I have replaced
discovery with past attachment,
when I have trusted in narrow perspective
over Your expansive vision.

Give me a questioning openness
to both the familiar and unfamiliar.
May I revisit the world with Your eyes.   AMEN

Evening Prayer

For surprises that land
with the force of Newton's apple;
for risks that unsettle
the everyday management of dullness;
for change that feels unwelcome
until it's embraced;
I give You thanks,
God of the shock,
God of customary reformation.   AMEN

Scripture Readings

Ecclesiastes 1:16–2:12, 2:21–26   *Chasing the wind*
1 Corinthians 13:8–13   *What lasts?*

Blessing

Your blessing when freed from past burdens;
Your blessing when we feel their weight.
Your blessing in the joy of new discoveries;
Your blessing when they become double-edged.
Your blessing when doors open to the future.
Your blessing when they close before and behind us. AMEN

THE WAY WITHIN

*The inner journey
and spiritual orientation
towards God and the world.*

*Create in me a clean heart,
O God,
and put a new and right spirit
within me.*

~ Proverbs 3:6 ~

Prayer

Do not worry about anything,
but in everything by prayer and supplication
with thanksgiving let your requests
be made known to God.

~ Philippians 4:6 ~

Meditation

I came looking for God
When I was in **P**ain …
When I wanted to **R**eflect …
When I was feeling **A**ngry …
When my spirit was **Y**earning …
When I was feeling **E**xhilarated …
When I was filled with **R**emorse …
When my soul was **F**rightened …
When I could not **U**nderstand …
When my heart was full of **L**ove …

And I found that God was already here
with me,
surrounding me,
comforting me,
confronting me,
forgiving me,
understanding me,
and holding me in prayerful love.

Whenever I'm feeling prayerful
and whenever I'm not,
no matter where I am
or whenever I forget,
God is already with me
holding me in prayerful love.

Morning Prayer (Psalm 139:1–12)

O Lord, You have searched me and known me.
You know when I sit down and when I rise up;
You discern my thoughts from far away.
You search out my path and my lying down,
and are acquainted with all my ways.

Even before a word is on my tongue,
O Lord, You know it completely.
You hem me in, behind and before,
and lay Your hand upon me.
Such knowledge is too wonderful for me;
it is so high that I cannot attain it.
Where can I go from Your spirit?
Or where can I flee from Your presence?
If I ascend to heaven, You are there;
if I make my bed in Sheol, You are there.
If I take the wings of the morning
and settle at the farthest limits of the sea,
even there Your hand shall lead me,
and Your right hand shall hold me fast.
If I say, 'Surely the darkness shall cover me,
and the light around me become night',
even the darkness is not dark to You;
the night is as bright as the day,
for darkness is as light to You.   AMEN

Evening Prayer

Help me to set aside this day, O God;
to leave behind the stresses and worries,
to treasure the moments of joy
and release the sting of bitterness.
Prepare my soul for sleep
that I may awake refreshed and renewed
to face the opportunities and challenges
of a new day.   AMEN

Scripture Readings

Philippians 4:4–9   *Instructions to the Philippians*
Matthew 6:1–14   *Jesus teaches his disciples about
prayer*

Blessing

May the Peace of God surround me,
the Grace of God astound me,
the Hope of God ground me,
and the Love of God abound in me.   AMEN

Meditation

Let the words of my mouth and the meditation of my heart
be acceptable to you, O Lord, my rock and my redeemer.

~ Psalm 19:14 ~

Meditation

I find my favourite spot
and make myself comfortable.
I close my eyes,
take a deep breath,
and plunge into the depths of my being.
Time slows ...
    then falters ...
        then stands still.
And slowly,
the world around me,
starts to dissolve away
as I empty the In-Tray of my day.

All distractions melt
as I retreat deeper into myself
and just when I think I can't go any further inwards
I start to blossom out
into the wide open spaces of my soul.

And here in this miraculous space
I can see, and sense, and feel
all that I am
and all that I can be.
It is here that I wrestle and play
with God.
It is here that I refresh my soul
before I resurface again
to the ticking of the clock,
ready for the tasks that await.

Morning Prayer

Living, loving God,
help me to set times and spaces apart this day

for me to meet with You.
And in between those times
be the breath behind my words,
the impulse behind my actions
and the reason behind my thoughts.   AMEN

Evening Prayer

Help me to meditate on this day past, O God.
Let me unpack and lay before You
the thoughts of my mind
and the intentions of my heart.

Help me to reflect
on what I have said and done
and what I could have done better.

And help me to learn from this day
and grow faithfully for tomorrow.   AMEN

Scripture Readings

> Psalm 19   *Proclaiming the glory of God*
> Mark 1:35–38   *Jesus prays*

Blessing

> God above.
> God around.
> God within.   AMEN

Identity

'Who do you say I am?'

~ Mark 8:29a ~

Meditation

The world walks past
as I sit in my chair and watch.
Every so often the light will change
and the large window acts like a mirror.
Not sure I like what I see.
Stories unfold throughout the day.
But which stories will I believe?

The light can play tricks,
tell lies about your age.
Makeup covers wrinkles and blemishes.
I judge you from my chair,
scoffing at all the disguises.

It's not as if my scars are there for all to see.
I wonder, would a heart on my sleeve be more honest
than the ink on yours?

But then,
in between your lines,
a story –
a story, that needs to be read with care,
a story that needs to be told,
heard,
shared.

Morning Prayer

O God,
help me to remember
that others have looked in the mirror this morning,
and prayed for strength.
The strength not to cover up their scars,
the marks that perhaps define them,
but to wear them with pride.

Hopeful that, as others see them,
They, too, may have the courage
to be honest,
to be open
to a new story
and a new truth this day.   AMEN

Evening Prayer

Lord,
as I wipe away the memory of today
and put my layers back into the wardrobe,
help me to shed the false ideas
of who I am.
Let my lullaby
be Your voice of love.
Help me to rest
in Your arms of peace, O Lord,
knowing that I am fully known.
And let me, when I wake
remember who You ask me to be.   AMEN

Scripture Readings

Mark 8:29a   *'But what about you?' he asked. 'Who do you say I am?'*

Psalm 139:14   *I am fearfully and wonderfully made*

Blessing

May the marks we leave
on each other this day,
be those of love, peace and grace.   AMEN

Incarnation

She gave birth to her first born son and wrapped him in bands of cloth.

~ Luke 2:7 ~

Meditation

I held him when he was a baby,
just back from their home town,
days old, infinitely precious,
tiny toes
tiny fingers
I could count every single one.

There was always something special about him,
unique, even –
a little boy, running about the place
yet with an expression
that almost said he'd been here before.

The mischief grew up
and matured into something different;
a boy who taught like a man,
a man, who laughed like a boy.

Some said he would be trouble,
that his cavalier attitude would catch up with him,
but it was his depth,
his ability to call it like he saw it
and his love
that was so dangerous.

And as I watch Him now,
His breathing ragged
His suffering great
bleeding,
dying.

Bloodied toes,
bloodied fingers –
I could count every single one

Incarnation –
God Himself
with us.

Morning Prayer

God of life,
midwife of our lives,
You bring about change and possibility,
delivering life itself
in Your Son.
Be with us this new day.

Evening Prayer

God of the lengthening shadows,
You chose to live our life with us;
You are with us in all that we have.
In Your Son, Jesus,
You sought to understand.
Draw this day to its right conclusion
ready for a new day.   AMEN

Scripture Readings

Luke 2   *The birth of Christ*
Luke 23   *The death of Christ*

Blessing

In the birth of Christ
may God come to you;
may God be born in your life today;
may God transform you and our world
by the power of His love.   AMEN

Gender

So God created humankind in God's own image,
in the image of God they were created;
male and female God created them.

~ Genesis 1:27 (NRSV abridged) ~

Meditation

Elohim
is Hebrew:
one of the words used
since the start of our time
to name and address God.

Elohim
is a plural term
describing male and female
in One True God.

Elohim
is Creator
bestowing gender
so that each one made
should reflect part
of the mystery of the Whole.

Elohim
is Soul Nurturer
feeding the masculine and the feminine
at the deepest level within us
inviting us to be
as She and He has gifted us to be.

Morning Prayer

Thank You, God,
for the journey of gender
and the special relationships
that gender makes possible.

Thank You for marriage,
for sex as an act of complete love,
and for deep platonic friendships
that are enriched by
the differences of gender.

Thank You for Your example
of wholeness.
Please bless this day
those who will experience brokenness
persecution or prejudice
because of their perceived gender.
May they know in their hearts
that they are Your children
reflecting an integral part of You.   AMEN

Evening Prayer

From the beginning,
the Spirit, Ruach,
is feminine –
She who creates at Your Word.

The Word becomes Your Son,
Jesus,
who is masculine –
He who teaches and heals.

The Teacher lifted women up
according them dignity and value
empowering their faith
and honouring their gifts.

The Teacher humbled self-righteous men
according them humility and self-awareness,
disempowering their arrogance and hypocrisy
that they should discover the truth.

Now the Spirit lives and works in every gender
enabling our search for
authenticity, integrity and wholeness.
Bless You, God, for male and female spirituality.   AMEN

Scripture Readings

Genesis 1:26–31   *God makes humankind*
Galatians 3:19–29   *We are one in Christ Jesus*

Blessing

Go as God's child.
Rejoice in your gender.
Celebrate the diversity of humankind.
Seek the wholeness of God
alone and in loving community
that serves to reflect Elohim.   AMEN

PRAYER NOTES

Forgiveness

Then Peter came and said to him,
'Lord, if another member of the church sins against me,
how often should I forgive? As many as seven times?'
Jesus said to him,
'Not seven times, but, I tell you, seventy-seven times.'

~ Matthew 18:21–22 ~

Meditation

Jesus was a hard man;
took no prisoners;
called a spade a spade;
didn't let folk waffle;
was highly sensitive to hypocrisy
and spoke some harsh truth.
But when he spoke of forgiveness
and then went on
to practise what he preached,
he raised the bar
way beyond what most of us
are capable of reaching.
And it's not just about ability –
it's about the will to forgive.
Quite frankly,
I'd rather go on living with resentment
than roll over and forgive.
I'd rather hold on to that edge of anger
than gather the energy
to have another go at building a bridge.
The work of forgiveness
demands too much energy.
It seems easier just to move on
and chalk it up to experience.
But Jesus was a hard man.
He didn't simply roll over.
He didn't simply smile sweetly
and allow others
to go on hurting,
to go on betraying.
He lifted forgiveness up to God

in an agonising cry:
'Father forgive'.
And, if we can do no other ...
if the time for building bridges is past,
if the time for enduring more hurt has expired,
we call on God to do the work that we can't,
and we move on –
singed,
perhaps a tiny bit broken
and certainly scarred;
and we find our healing
in the love and forgiveness of God.

Morning Prayer

God, as I awake, with that churning in my stomach,
with that ball of tension,
make me stop just for a moment,
to examine what it is.
Let me ask whether I am carrying anger or resentment
that I could lay down.
Show me how destructive these emotions are.
Remind me of the power I allow them to have,
and help me to resolve to let go –
to let go and let God
and in letting go, help me to be free.   AMEN

Evening Prayer

God of infinite love and patience,
thank You for all the times today
when You forgave my shortcomings
and for all those times You enabled me
to forgive others.
Lord, there's a cathartic power
in being able to forgive.
It lightens my spirit, puts a spring in my step,
and there is joy in the knowledge
that forgiveness is not a limited commodity.
Like love, it never runs out.
Like love, it sets me free.
Like love, it is a gift from You.   AMEN

Scripture Readings

Hosea 14:4–9   *The ways of the Lord are right*
Matthew 18:21–35   *How often should I forgive?*

Blessing

May the God of all forgiveness free you this day
and enable you to freely forgive others
in the name of the Father, the Son and the Holy Spirit.
    AMEN

PRAYER NOTES

Grace

The grace of our Lord poured out on me abundantly.

~ 1 Timothy 1:14 ~

Meditation

Without merit,
we receive.
You give freely and abundantly,
pouring out like a waterfall,
cascading over us
yet
always graceful
moving with elegance
dancing
in and around and through.

The divine benevolence –
a gift for us to unwrap,
perhaps with abandon,
like an excited child at Christmas.
Perhaps layer by layer.

Slowly

Carefully
with each tear imprinting deeper and deeper,
so as to save our souls.

It is one thing to understand it,
but an entirely different thing
to give or to experience.
Sometimes it's hard to imagine
a way of being, so deep rooted,
surpassing all that our mind, heart, soul and strength
can offer.
But this way, this grace,
is what we are given
and is what we are to give.

Now we see.
Now we hear.

Morning Prayer

Sometimes we just don't feel like it.
Other times we plainly don't want to.
Every now and again we can't help it.
Every moment of every day we need it.

Help us gracious God,
to be generous in our giving,
to be humble in our receiving.
Let us be at all times full of grace,
whether we feel like it, want to, or not.
Give us gifts of grace that we might unwrap them
and share them with all we meet today.   AMEN

Evening Prayer

When did I give today?
When did I receive today?
When did I encounter Your Grace?

Did I see it,
perhaps sense it?
Did I speak it,
or hear it whispered?

Help me, Lord,
to know Your grace,
to recognise it,
in the giving
and receiving.   AMEN

Scripture Readings

I Timothy 1:12–20	*The grace of our Lord poured out on me abundantly*
John 1:14–18	*Grace and truth came through Jesus Christ*

Blessing

May the grace of the Lord Jesus Christ,
and the love of God,
and the fellowship of the Holy Spirit
be with you all.   AMEN

Stillness

'Be still, and know that I am God!
I am exalted among the nations, I am exalted in the earth.'
The Lord of hosts is with us; the God of Jacob is our refuge.

~ Psalm 46:10–11 ~

Meditation

Stillness is frightening.
Like nakedness,
it leaves me exposed
with nowhere to hide.
I'm alone,
with my mind
and in my mind.
Only God is there
in the terrible stillness,
sharing it with me,
hearing my thoughts,
knowing me completely.

And yet, despite the fear,
it is this for which my soul aches,
for which my spirit cries out:
to be still in God's presence,
being fully known,
and held in his indescribable love.

In the stillness,
in the holding,
God's love assures me
that I am understood,
that my motives are known,
that I am forgiven.
No more need to hide the things
that fill me with shame.

In the stillness,
before the Holy One,
God in Three Persons,
I know I belong.

Morning Prayer

Thank You, God of the morning,
that I am fully known by You.
By this I am set free
to be still before You.
There is nothing hidden away
that could ever separate me from You.

How different I am, Lord.
I learn about a blot
in someone's copybook of life,
and I find it difficult to understand,
never mind to forgive.
Instead, I judge, and I condemn,
and love no longer has a chance.

Forgive me, Lord,
and remind me today,
in the still moments,
that Your love is there for me,
unconditionally.
And give me the strength to love others
with Your love.
In Jesus' name.   AMEN

Evening Prayer

Holy God,
Several times today
I heard Your voice say to me,
'Peace; be still.'
I heard You say,
'Come and bring your worries,
your mistakes,
your troubles,
into the stillness I provide for you.
Come to me and rest.'
Thank You, God.

I'm reminded of the many in our world
for whom stillness is but a distant dream.
They live in places of war and upheaval,

of injustice and despair.
Some need to hide,
day after day, night after night,
in flimsy shelters
where there is no peace.

Holy One, how can this be changed?
How can peace be found in this troubled world?
Help Your people to be peacemakers,
so that all may be able to be still
in Your presence,
and be embraced by Your love,
this night, and for ever.
For Jesus' sake.   AMEN

Scripture Readings

| Psalm 46 | *Stillness before God* |
| Mark 4:35–41 | *Stillness with Jesus* |

Blessing

May you find rest in the stillness of God,
the Blessed Trinity of Love,
day after day, and night after night,
for ever more.   AMEN

PRAYER NOTES

Lament

The sacrifice acceptable to God is a broken spirit;
a broken and contrite heart, O God, you will not despise.

~ Psalm 51:17 ~

Meditation

Sadness,
devastating sadness fills my heart
as I look at our world.
Nation is at war with nation;
death and destruction
of the cruellest kind
are all around,
and hope has lost its way.

Despair,
I see crushing despair
among people who
ought to be one.
Neighbour is at war with neighbour;
hatred rears its ugly head
and drives folk from their homes
into a future of anguish and pain,
or no future at all.

Sorrow,
overwhelming sorrow
threatens to take away my breath.
My right hand is at war with my left hand;
thoughts are jumbled within me.
Regret and worry fight for space
where calm and peace ought to be,
but they have fled.

Out of the depth I cry for help,
in my brokenness,
to the One who is familiar with sorrow
and acquainted with grief.
I cry for help
for the world,

for neighbours,
for myself.
Lord of peace, come quickly.

Morning Prayer

Some mornings, Lord, I'm too afraid
to turn on the news or read the papers.
Some mornings I'd rather ignore
what is happening on the earth.
And yet, You call us to see what's around us
with Your eyes,
and to love one another
with Your kind of love.
On this new day, Lord,
help me to have hope.
Help me to discover ways
of finding peace in my own life,
and give me the courage
to reach out to others
with compassion and love,
for Jesus' sake.   AMEN

Evening Prayer

God,
the day has passed
and nothing much seems to have changed,
at least not where wars and violence are concerned.
Again, news stories have unsettled me,
stories of harm and hurt and heartbreak.
Lord, how can it be
that human beings will not
live and let live.

But sometimes I hear different talk,
I hear stories of compassion,
of courage, of care for others.
I learn of love
for those who are desolate.
Thank You, Lord, for the peacemakers.
Thank You also

for making peace within me,
so I can lie down to sleep
trusting myself into Your loving arms.
In Jesus' name.   AMEN

Scripture Readings

Psalm 51	*David's lament*
Isaiah 52:13 – 53:12	*The One who is broken*

Blessing

May the God of hope
fill you with all joy and peace in believing,
so that you may abound in hope
by the power of the Holy Spirit.   AMEN

~ Romans 14:13 ~

PRAYER NOTES

Disciplined

> *Know then in your heart*
> *that as a parent disciplines a child*
> *so the Lord your God disciplines you.*
>
> ~ Deuteronomy 8:5 ~

Meditation

Disciple and discipline –
same root –
learning, imitating,
practising the way of Jesus:
He who taught Your way of life,
He who corrected His followers,
He whom You sent
out of the root of Jesse.

Disciple and discipline –
a marriage of medium and message –
proclaiming, confessing, forgiving,
welcoming, healing, serving as Jesus did:
we who often get it wrong,
we who like to take the huff,
we who are fussy
about the company we keep.

Disciple and discipline –
a recipe for freedom in the Spirit –
praying, studying, worshipping,
loving You, others and ourselves:
Your children turning the other cheek,
Your children sharing their resources,
Your children growing from the true Vine
and bearing the fruits of Your Spirit.

Morning Prayer

Lord Jesus,
You rebuked Peter
for arguing against Your way of the cross.
You rebuked James and John

when they sought glory.
You rebuked the disciples
when they tried to hold back the little ones.

Today, Lord,
may I be a support, not a stumbling block
to those who make sacrifices for others.
May I seek to serve, not to dominate,
in my relationships and tasks.
May I be a welcomer, not a shunner,
of vulnerable ones who seek Your company.
Today, Lord,
may it be the Christ in me
that others see.   AMEN

Evening Prayer

Divine Accountant,
I submit to You, the sums of my day:
Here is how I spent my time ......
Here is how I used my gifts ......
Here is how I spent my money ......
Here is how I related to others ......
Receive my offerings, Lord.
Encourage and correct me.
Bless my discipleship.
Strengthen my discipline.
And lead me towards wholeness
for the sum of the whole
is so much greater than its parts.   AMEN

Scripture Readings

Deuteronomy 8:1–6   *The reason for God's discipline*
Hebrews 12:1–13   *The example of Jesus for disciples*

Blessing

> Act justly, child of God,
> love tenderly, child of God,
> walk humbly with Him, child of God,
> for this is what is required of you
> who already know God's blessings.   AMEN

Resistance

Because of all the trouble this widow is giving me,
I will see to it that she gets her rights.

~ Luke 18:5a ~

Meditation

Easter has been cancelled,
becomes a Bank Holiday.

No need to taunt the dead
with resurrection.

He has protest in mind
but takes time out

from everyday collapse.
He forks corn from a can.

The mob's rage, he believes,
raised the crucified

three days later;
the resurrection required

a hammering fury,
not this acquiescence:

the banks' hate mail
is now a status symbol;

people offer their mouths
as personalised ATMs.

He kicks a lamppost.
The mob has been cancelled.

His toe is broken.
Still, he must resist.

Morning Prayer

God, here I am again, all ready
to bombard You with petitions!

But I think I will shut myself up
for once, and instead listen
to Your voice in the widow
raging against the unjust judge,
kicking at his reinforced doors,
pelting his windows with pebbles.
I will join You today in rage
and kick and pelt, and seek
to answer my own typical prayers.

Evening Prayer

There's no end to disaster.
　　When one finishes, another starts
　　　　and, if not, the newspapers
　　　　　　and friends on social media
　　　　　　　　will invent one more thing
　　　　　　　　　　for me to get cross about.

　　　　　　　　There's no end to distraction.
　　　　　　　Tonight, help me to focus,
　　　　　　to sleep on what matters
　　　　　and so tomorrow make
　　　　the difference between
despair and hope.

Scripture Readings

　　　　Jeremiah 1:11–19　　*Get yourself ready!*
　　　　　　Luke 18:1–6　　*The persistent widow*

Blessing

　　　　　　May God bless the shy ones
　　　　　　with persistence.
　　　　　　May God bless the tub-thumpers
　　　　　　with reticence.
　　　　　　And bless both doubly
　　　　　　when they reticently persist.

Vulnerability

And a woman in the city, who was a sinner, having learned that he was eating in the Pharisee's house, brought an alabaster jar of ointment. She stood behind him at his feet, weeping, and began to bathe his feet with her tears and to dry them with her hair. Then she continued kissing his feet and anointing them with the ointment.

~ Luke 7:37–38 ~

Meditation

Fragile, but not broken,
naked, but never ashamed,
I am laid bare.

Maybe that's it;
when you open yourself so wide
there is nowhere to hide.

That's when you find out who you are.
That's when you understand.
Trust

Morning Prayer

Courage

It's not that I lack confidence per se
but who is willing to be the lone voice,
the first to speak out,
the hand that reaches out
and touches the leper,
the one that stands
in solidarity?
Lord, I wish it could be me
So, courage!
That's what I ask for today
so that I can be vulnerable.

Evening Prayer

What do I see
when I look in the mirror,

when I take off my suit,
my uniform,
peel off all that I wore today.
Who do I see?
Help me Lord, to see me as You do
precious,
a beloved child of God –
not as the choices
or the mistakes I made
but as the child You love;
and as I rest in You
fill me with Your love
for the children I will
see tomorrow.

Scripture Readings

Luke 7:36–50	*Jesus anointed by a sinful woman*
Psalm 121	*Where do I find my strength?*

Blessing

May all that you do and say
reflect the love and tenderness
that the Lord our God shows you
in every moment.

May all that I do and say
reflect the love and tenderness
that the Lord, my God, shows me
in every moment.

Dependent/Independent

For freedom, Christ has set us free.

~ Galatians 5:1 ~

Meditation

With Sinatra, I feel an urge to do it
my way, even though my way is hardly
unique and follows a script written
strictly in advance.

DNA, delivery, wrapped in sheets
or dumped on a doorstep, breast or bottle,
held close or left to cry, given love or only
what money buys:

it all adds up to subtract from what
I think is freedom. My independence
is dependent on the dark matter
lost to memory,

the past my future is rooted in,
grows from, and can't be shed like skin.
But God is rooted there too,
the light the darkness

cannot put out, the alpha and omega
book-binding my life and every life;
Stuff Sinatra! He didn't know himself.
Let God write me …

Morning Prayer

God of surprises,
Every morning, I do so many things
without thinking about them!
I brew two morning coffees, read
some poems so I think in lines,
write for a while, make my daughter
a packed lunch, pack her off
to school, open the email.

God of surprises, sometimes
You must yawn at my life.
I couldn't complain if You
switched off and watched
paint dry instead. Help me,
between routines, to waken
You up, to surprise myself
by small acts of love or faith
that redirect the day.   AMEN

Evening Prayer

God of freedom, I am no puppet
    and You are not pulling strings.
You have sent me today neither
    to heaven nor hell. I've blundered
and You've left me to clear up
    the mess. Flames rise from
the war-torn town. You do not
    blow them out. My cry rises
to the silence, my prayer rises
    to You like a burnt offering.   AMEN

Scripture Readings

Jonah 4:1–11	*Jonah's frustration*
Galatians 5:1–6, 13–14	*Freedom in Christ*

Blessing

May our celebrations be unstaged,
our compliments unpolitical,
our generosity without guile,
our hope without impatience.
Bless us that we be as surprised
as water becoming wine.   AMEN

Exile

Then one of them, when he saw that he was healed,
turned back, praising God with a loud voice;
and he fell on his face at Jesus' feet, giving him thanks.
And he was a Samaritan.

~ Luke 17:15–16 ~

Meditation

Sometimes it takes the outsider
to really see,
to grasp the momentum
of an occasion,
to gauge the impact
with accuracy.
It takes someone
outside of the crowd
to pick up the cues.
When those on the inside
are too busy
being blinded by tradition
and expectation,
the outsider
grasps the import
and closes in
to maximise the potential
and realise the blessing.
Fresh eyes
go a long way
to bringing new perspective
and alerting others
to the miracles
being played out
right in our midst.
Sometimes 'the foreigner'
just gets it,
bringing fresh vision
and renewed energy.
May we look
for those moments

when 'foreigners'
show us the way.

Morning Prayer

God, often we simply go through the motions,
do the things we've always done.
We treat the familiar with contempt,
no longer moved by wonder,
and only when things are taken from us
are we stirred into action,
or when we see what we think of as our entitlement
handed on to others.
God help us to appreciate all that we have
and the fresh perspective that others bring.
May we operate with a spirit of generosity,
thankful for new insights
and always be willing to learn
from the most unlikely teachers.
You, who did not abandon your people in exile
enlarge our hearts today
until we can welcome
the stranger in our midst.   AMEN

Evening Prayer

Lord, we pray this night,
for rest and relaxation,
in the place that we call home.
We bring to You all those
who are considered outsiders –
far from family,
far from all that is familiar.
In all that we do, help us to be prepared
to make room for others,
to share our material and spiritual wealth.
And, more than that, help us to be aware
of how we are enriched by being open
to all that others bring.
May our horizons be expanded
as we open ourselves to others
discovering the presence of Christ in all.   AMEN

Scripture Readings

Ezra 6:19–22	*The Passover is celebrated in exile*
Luke 17:11–19	*The foreigner returns to praise God*

Blessing

Be enriched as you bring enrichment.
Be accommodated as you make room for others.
Find the blessing of the God of all
as you bless the exile and the stranger.   AMEN

PRAYER NOTES

Poor in Spirit

Oh my son Absalom, my son, my son Absalom! Would that I had died instead of you. O Absalom, my son, my son.

~ 2 Samuel 18:33 ~

Meditation

See him sitting there
between two gates –
life and death.

All of his own making,
all of his own destroying,
waiting for news.

Oh, King David,
you made your bed,
you ruined your boy.

There he is –
pierced to a tree
between heaven and earth.

The news comes;
the battle is won,
but your boy is gone.

Your victory as a king,
your failure as a father
breaks you.

Rich beyond belief
but in grief
so poor in spirit.

Another Son is there
pierced to a tree
between heaven and earth.

Redeeming you
Restoring you
Dying, instead of you.

Pouring blessings on you
When you are poor in spirit.

Morning Prayer

Blessed are we who know our need of God.
Blessed are we who know our own fragility,
our own mortality,
our utter dependence on the One
who has given us life,
the One
to whom all life returns.
Blessed are we
when stripped of all pretension and illusion
we crave the company of God.

Lord God,
my hands are empty,
my mind is open
my heart is broken for You.
Keep me in Your communion
and bind me eternally to the ones I love.

Evening Prayer

Bless O Lord, all whose spirit is troubled:
by depths of despair or grief,
by loss that seems insurmountable
by guilt that gives them no rest.
Bless O Lord all whose spirit is hostage
to wealth, to property, to power-seeking
all for their own name's sake
with no regard for the poor.
Bless O Lord, all whose spirit is Christ-like.
Bless all who live Your Kingdom now.
AMEN

Scripture Readings

2 Samuel 18	*David battles against Absalom*
Matthew 5:1–13	*The Beatitudes*

Blessing

> May the blessing of God be on you,
> in your poverty, in your sadness
> in your hunger, in your mercy
> in your purity, in your peacemaking
> and in your persecution.   AMEN

PRAYER NOTES

Sacrificial

*But when Christ had offered for all time a single sacrifice for sins,
he sat down at the right hand of God.*

~ Hebrews 10:12 ~

Meditation

Cenotaph – empty tomb;
See it lying there, still, silent,
enveloping the
broken dreams
broken bodies
broken lives
of an entire generation.

A stark contrast to the euphoria
of the flag-waving crowd
that sent them to end all wars.

Lifetimes before,
another tomb lies empty
another victim of a violent death

but here
the death and violence
is the beginning
not the end
filled not with despair
but hope
breaking the grip of humanity's violence,

showing a glimpse of perfection
tempered by the darkness of reality
the making of all things new
that will exist
when violence
is no more.

Today,
let us amidst terror
kindle the flame
of hope

that
Christ shows us –
a new way within.

Morning Prayer

In the shards of the morning's light
may we glimpse a moment of the divine;
may we see in the dawn
Your light that shines in the world;
may we live out Your Kingdom
and find Your way within.   AMEN

Evening Prayer

Sometimes we are so overwhelmed
by the hopelessness of violence.
We live in a world where terror is real
and the cost is on our doorstep.
Give us peace when we are disturbed;
may we respond with love
and hate to retaliate.   AMEN

Scripture Readings

Hebrews 10   *Christ's sacrifice is for all time*
Romans 6:13   *Offer yourself as an instrument of*
righteousness

Blessing

The world is ours for a time,
may we be encouraged to know it;
the human mind is ours for a time,
may we be encouraged to explore it and expand it;
the human heart beats out its number for a time,
may we be encouraged to be fully alive in our time.
May peace be with us and our world this day.   AMEN

THE WAY AMONG

The relationships, way of being and practice
of the faith community
in their common journey towards God
and reaching out
to the wider unchurched community.

All who believed were together and had all things in common;
they would sell their possessions and goods and distribute the
*   proceeds to all as any had need.*
Day by day as they spent much time together in the temple,
they broke bread at home
and ate their food with glad and generous hearts,
praising God and having the goodwill of the people.

~ Acts 2:44–47a ~

Worship

I will not listen to the melody of your harps.
But let justice roll down like waters.

~ Amos 5:23–24 ~

Meditation

Here is the song of the woman
who will not listen
to the lies and fudgery
of grey officialdom.
She will not see 'common sense'
She will not be 'reasonable'
when people are hungry
or thirsty or homeless.
Her song is a waterfall roar.
The officials strum their harps
but they can't block her out.
They buy in drum-kits,
a forty-strong orchestra,
a mile-high stack of amplifiers.
They create toe-curling feedback,
hammer in earplugs,
climb to the top of Everest,
but they can't block her out.
When she talks, they shout;
when she whispers, they sleep;
when she tells them to wake up
and make things happen, they sing
'All Things Bright and Beautiful'.
But her hymn is a waterfall roar
and soon there are other waterfalls,
all of them roaring together,
bright and beautiful together
in worship of God.

Morning Prayer

I cannot always find the words I need.
My voice does not always sound
like music to my ears.

I am distracted by traffic noise,
notifications on my mobile phone,
the soap operas of my own life
spinning around my brain.

Lord God,
may there be moments today
of encounter with You,
when the racket falls silent
and even I stop talking
and instead know You as God
in whoever I am with,
in justice I help create,
in wordless praise
and silent psalms.   AMEN

Evening Prayer

Whether I am alone or with others,
I thank You that You welcome
imperfect voices like mine
daring to raise themselves
to the level of prayer.
May what I sing in church,
the words of prayers,
the Bible's awkward insights,
be mirrored in the worship
of my everyday life
in rooms, kitchens and streets.

Scripture Readings

Amos 5:21–24	*The day of the Lord*
Hebrews 10:19–25	*Draw near to God*

Blessing

God's blessing be on your out-of-tune harps
that they might sing anew.
God's blessing be on your attempts to live justly
that they might bring a new song
to the lips of those
who have not yet used their voices.   AMEN

Gathered

The crowds that went ahead of him and that followed were shouting,
'Hosanna to the Son of David!
Blessed is the one who comes in the name of the Lord!
Hosanna in the highest heaven!'

~ Matthew 21:9 ~

Meditation

Blessed is the one who comes in the Name of the Lord
– a cry taken up by ordinary folk,
men, women, children
out lining the streets
looking for a spectacle,
longing for a cause.
Blessed is the one who comes in the Name of the Lord
– a cry to get behind,
to celebrate,
to champion,
welcoming the rebel
on whom the hopes of a nation are pinned.
Blessed is the one who comes in the Name of the Lord
– a cry to imitate
when there is little else to do
and nowhere else to be,
when it is easier
to go along with the crowd.
Blessed is the one who comes in the Name of the Lord
– a cry that echoes in emptiness
when enthusiasm wanes
and hope fades,
when excitement moves aside
to make way for disillusionment.
Blessed is the one who comes in the Name of the Lord
– a cry that drifts away
on the tide of change
as the mood of the crowd
becomes blacker
and more dangerous.

Blessed is the one who comes in the Name of the Lord
– a cry that becomes mocking
as the people jeer
and change their tune
and Blessed
becomes Crucify!
Blessed is the one who comes in the Name of the Lord

Morning Prayer

Lord God, we thank You today
for freedom of will and of thought.
We thank You for infinite possibility.
Forgive us when we limit ourselves
to the tried and the tested,
when we are too timid to be different,
to go against the crowd.
Forgive us when we are easily led into
things we'd rather avoid.
Give us this day
the resolve to make a difference,
to confound expectations,
to refuse to run with the crowd
and step out boldly
knowing that You are beside us
every step of the way.   AMEN

Evening Prayer

God, sometimes today we felt lonely.
Sometimes we felt isolated
because we refused to do what is popular
or what was expected.
It's easier just to go with the flow.
Standing out takes courage.
But just when we felt the urge
to turn back to the safety of the crowd
You showed up
and helped us to remain strong.
In our rest, may we know contentment
that comes from leaving the fickle crowd
to be gathered into Your community.   AMEN

Scripture Readings

Numbers 11:4–11	*The Israelites complain in the wilderness*
Matthew 21:1–11	*The crowds hail Jesus*

Blessing

The blessing of God
who calls us out from the crowd
and releases us into wondrous discovery
along the path of life
be yours every step of the way.   AMEN

PRAYER NOTES

Welcome

And if you greet only your brothers and sisters,
what more are you doing than others?
Do not even the Gentiles do the same?

~ Matthew 5:47 ~

Meditation

I receive 'Good morning' and a smile,
as a book and neatly folded sheet of paper
are thrust into my hands,
before she turns to continue her conversation
with someone she knows.

Where do I go? Where can I sit?

I usher myself inside
and find a seat that looks safe,
away from the eyes of inquisitive stares.

Will I know when to stand and sit,
... or kneel
and what to say and sing
... and when?

And afterwards,
the awkwardness of conversation
as one by one they greet me
with the same questions
then shuffle off,
relieved to have done their duty
and made their escape.

Outside, the same sign
still hangs in pride of place –
ALL ARE WELCOME.

And I wonder ...
as I wander homewards.

Morning Prayer

Gracious God,
help us to realise
that welcome is more than a word:
that it runs deeper than a cup of tea
and lasts longer than a smile.

Help us to see that welcome
is a way of being
and not a task to be done.

Help us to rejoice in the presence
of fellow guests in Your house;
to see them as companions
and not strangers;
to hear their stories
and see to their needs.

Help us to welcome others
as You welcome us.   AMEN

Evening Prayer

Loving God,
You have made a place for everyone
in Your house
and in Your heart.

You welcome us all
into Your presence
in the knowledge
that this is where we belong.

Help us to see
the spaces beside us,
for others to be
in Your presence too;
and give us the faith
to fill them
by inviting others in.   AMEN

Scripture Readings

Matthew 5:43–48   *Loving beyond boundaries*
Matthew 25:31–46   *Judged on our treatment of others*

Blessing

May God embrace you
in your coming
and in your going;
in your journeying
and in your welcome home.   AMEN

PRAYER NOTES

Inclusion

Send her away. She is following us and making all this noise!
~ Matthew 15:23b ~

Meditation

The greater the divisions we create,
the greater our efforts at unity.

You will be stakeholders in society
and pay off our luxurious debt.

When cracks widen to people-size,
we press for low-budget repairs.

What isn't improved by a smile,
by the appearance of tolerance!

Come on in! The door is wide open!
We'll be sure to bolt it behind us.

We stretch out our palms
to push you back to sea.

We dump a doormat, raise a sign.
You know you've been welcome.

Morning Prayer

This morning, as with all mornings,
I have power to discriminate
between love and hate,
between right and wrong,
between lesser evil and possible good,
between grey and grey.
It is impossible for me
never to make judgements.
It is often undesirable
to remain safely balanced
or cling to a rocking fence.
But may my choices be informed
by Your forgiving love;
may my prejudices be clear

and be overcome;
may my compassion be real
and not merely appear that way.   AMEN

Evening Prayer

I wanted to include everyone.
I wanted to make room in the inn,
to unlock doors, to love the hateful,
to embrace the least embraceable.
But while it's easy for me to include
people like me and to use exactly
the right words of invitation,
my churchy welcome has sometimes
made people feel more alone
than when they really were alone.
Forgive me; give me warmth, integrity
and the courage to risk welcoming
all those whom people like me
would rather kept their distance.   AMEN

Scripture Readings

      Micah 5:2–5a   *To the ends of the earth*
   Matthew 15:21–28   *A woman's faith*

Blessing

      All who gather
      crumbs from Your table;
      all who see themselves
      as dogs, pigs, scroungers;
      may Your words of love
      be a blessing
      as they sit down at Your feast.   AMEN

Queer

Then he (Jesus) went home, and the crowd came together again,
so that they could not even eat.
When the family heard it, they went out to restrain him,
for people were saying, 'He has gone out of his mind.'

~ Mark 3:21–22 ~

Meditation

It's a queer way of life
being a leper:
banished by temple leaders,
unclean for company
except our own,
this community of the contagious
one moment tending one another
the next scrapping for food or a blanket.

It's a queer way of life
being a eunuch:
whether mutilated or by nature
for we are destined to be alone
without partner or children
save for the company of our own
finding our faith together
and seeking solace in story sharing.

It's a queer way of life
being a disciple:
following a bizarre Rabbi
who makes us homeless, penniless,
jobless, and downright unpopular
except in the companionship of the poor,
the healing of the sick
and the breaking of bread round a table.

It's a queer way of life
when you challenge the norm.

Morning Prayer

Dear Lord,
it isn't normal
to love your enemies.
It isn't normal
to give all your money to the poor.
It isn't normal
to seek servitude instead of power.
It isn't normal
to travel life lightly.
In fact, Your lifestyle
is downright strange.
Today, and every day,
give me the courage
to challenge the norm.   AMEN

Evening Prayer

I have been thinking, Lord,
about all the people
I know who have the courage
to be true to who they are
even if it means being
thought strange or odd
or unfashionable
or unworthy.
Bless them.

I have been giving thanks, Lord,
for the friends I have
who encourage me
to live in the way
You ask of Your followers.
Bless them.

I have been wondering, Lord,
if people find me queer?
And if they don't,
is that because
I cannot be the self
that You created me to be?

Lord empower me to be counted
amongst the queer.   Amen

Scripture Readings

Mark 3:20–30   *Jesus is compared to Beelzebul*
John 6:60–66   *Disciples turn away from Jesus'*
                     teaching

Blessing

Look for the Christ in those you meet.
Recognise love among sisters and brothers.
Value the kindness of those who serve you.
See all humanity as the creation of God.   Amen

PRAYER NOTES

Holding Things in Common

All who believed were together and had all things in common.

~ Acts 2:44 ~

Meditation

Gathered together
bearing the pain
sharing the burden.
Stumbling over words of faith
that we believe
but nonetheless find hard to articulate.
Gathered together
bringing food
and offers of help
with practical things
like child care
or grocery shopping,
car maintenance
or transport.
Gathered together
allowing space to vent
and repeat the stories
and the memories
and the events
that preceded loss.
Gathered together
to comfort
and encourage
to embrace
and include.
Gathered together
breaking bread
and hoping
that in the broken pieces
we will know
the presence of God
broken with us
in the midst

of our community
broken and hurting together.
Gathered together
clinging to hope
praying for courage
feeling the love.

Morning Prayer

Parent God,
You created us to build a relationship
with You and with each other.
Forgive us when we isolate ourselves or others.
Open our hearts to know that we have much to share
and much to learn from others.
May we know the comfort and strength that comes
from sharing through joy or pain,
from leaning on and supporting one another.
In our work and in our worship,
may we build one another up,
sharing one another's hopes and fears
and bearing one another's burdens;
and, as we gather around Your word or at Your table
may we know Your healing and Your peace
affecting all that we do together and apart.   AMEN

Evening Prayer

God, we thank You
for all those who have ministered to us this day.
We thank You for bonds forged in worship
that spill over into our every day –
for all the reminders that, whenever we gather,
You are in our midst and, when we go out into the world,
You go with us.
We pray for all those who are alone this night:
those who are bereaved,
those who have no family,
those who have alienated others.
We pray for those who, even surrounded by others,
feel the ache of loneliness.
God of comfort and companionship,

draw near to all who need Your presence this night
and be near to us,
reminding us that Your love reaches us
wherever we are.   AMEN

Scripture Readings

>   Psalm 122   *The house of God*
>   Acts 2:43–47   *The early church community*

Blessing

> The God we find in the beauty of holiness
> accompany us into every gathering
> shedding presence and light
> in all of life.   AMEN

PRAYER NOTES

Learning Together

Therefore be imitators of God as dear children.
And walk in love,
as Christ also has loved us and given Himself for us.

~ Ephesians 5:1–2 ~

Meditation

As God's dear children
we will only learn
to imitate His voice –
together.

As God's dear children
we will only learn
to imitate Her actions –
together.

As God's dear children
we will only learn
to imitate His gentleness,
Her forgiveness,
His passion,
Her justice,
His mercy,
Her patience –
together.

So together,
may we learn to walk,
as Christ walked.
May we learn to love,
as Christ loved.
And may we learn to give,
as Christ gave himself for us,
that all things be brought
together.

Morning Prayer

Today, Lord God,
as we learn to follow in the footsteps,

of Christ who showed the way,
may we hear the cheers of joy
from the One who calls us 'child'.

Whether we rise to our feet
or fall flat on our faces;
whether we reach our destination
or trip along the way;
whether we hold the things that help us,
or grasp for something that makes us
totter and topple;
may we know that You are ever there,
not angry at our every stumble,
but delighting in our every step.   AMEN

Evening Prayer

Lord God,
thank You for the people
who taught me to walk further today,
than I was able to yesterday.

And so, tomorrow,
may I be the one
who helps someone to their feet,
teaches another their first steps,
encourages those who are weary,
binds the wounds of those who have fallen
or shoulders the heavy load
of those who carry many burdens.   AMEN

Scripture Readings

Ephesians 4:29 — 5:2   *Learning to live together*
1 Corinthians 13   *Learning to love together*

Blessing

The word of God to teach us,
the Son of God to hold us,
the Spirit of God to keep us
in the company of the saints,
with whom we learn new paths.   AMEN

Nurturing

People cannot love God, whom they have not seen,
if they do not love their brothers and sisters, whom they have seen.

~ 1 John 4:20b ~

Meditation

A friend of mine, a minister, worried
that theology professors in the pews
found his services intellectually thin.

But they came, not to argue,
but to encounter the Divine
and serve those around them.

Another friend, a woman of 23, who left
the church at 18 because her questions
were trivialised, still misses the buzz of
Sunday morning '*with her octogenarians*'.

Where else do people come together –
all ages, colours and life experiences –
to form a caring community?
Perhaps only in pubs, the kind of pubs
that are closing and being replaced
by Scandinavian-style hostelries
with designer beers and a clientele
charging devices, plugged into screens.

A church is a family, peppered with
impenetrable eccentrics, nippy sweeties,
know-it-alls, lost souls, our many selves:
all called, by God's sense of humour,
to love each other! And by that, to learn
how best to love God, made visible in
shared grief, laughter, words and silence,
in broken bodies and spilled blood.

Morning Prayer

May people I pass or meet today
be gifts to my soul. May those
I love easily strengthen my resolve

to love the difficult and awkward.
May I receive love unexpectedly
and accept it gladly. May the love
I have for You find its origin
in some depth and height
I barely understand,
but which remains like a petal
held in its root's invisible cradle.   AMEN

Evening Prayer

I thank You for everyone who,
even briefly, has given me a thought,
gift, smile, touch or embrace.
I pray for my family, whether
blood relatives, church members
or others who have reminded me
that we are children, fathered
and mothered by You. And so,
I pray for those from whom
I am estranged, and for those
I find strange, that I might yet
love them with all my heart
and soul and strength: love
built on the dust of the earth,
exactly where You wait for it.   AMEN

Scripture Readings

Deuteronomy 6:4–9   *Love the Lord your God*
1 John 4:16b–21   *God is Love*

Blessing

May bells ring
and organs play
and voices hymn
and joy be found
whenever the mould
forming on the world
is broken by love.   AMEN

Prophetic

John the baptiser appeared in the wilderness,
proclaiming a baptism of repentance for the forgiveness of sins.

~ Mark 1:4 ~

Meditation

They flocked to see him, this wild prophet.
Out of curiosity?
Out of novelty?
Out of boredom?
He was certainly a sight to behold
and he didn't mince his words.
He told it straight
dressed nothing up.
Yet, still folk wanted to listen,
maybe tired of being spoon fed
and molly-coddled.
They realised they needed to hear
something more challenging.
It wasn't a message of comfort
but, in a strange way,
it was a message of hope
and, somehow, the starkness
made it more real.
What if we stopped dressing up the story
and allowed the truth to emerge?
Being a messenger might involve
saying the things
that no one wants to hear
and showing a way
that no one wants to follow,
shaking folk out of their complacency
to look toward the light.

Morning Prayer

Lord, it's so easy for us to simply go with the flow,
to keep our heads down.
to keep out of the firing range –

anything for an easy life.
But we know that that is not where You call us to be.
You want us to stand up, to speak out,
to go beyond our comfort zones,
speaking truth in love.
Even if that makes us unpopular.
Lord, give us courage –
not massive amounts,
just a little so that we can try being prophetic today,
speaking Your word even when others don't want to hear it.
We thank You for all the contemporary examples we have
of those who chose to be prophetic:
Martin Luther King,
Oscar Romero,
Jane Haining,
Mother Teresa,
Desmond Tutu,
Malala Yousafzi –
just a few of those whose examples we follow.
Lord, help us to be prophets right where we are,
letting Your voice be heard in the places we frequent
for Your glory.   AMEN

Evening Prayer

Lord, it's been a long day
a day filled with so many emotions,
a day when we were conscious of You walking with us:
Your healing touch where there was division,
Your calming whisper where there was dissent,
Your persistent voice urging us to speak up
with Your word of promise.
It's not easy being a prophet, especially among our friends,
those who know us well.
But You call us to be non-conformists,
willing to stand up for those who are weak,
willing to speak up for those whose voices are not heard,
willing to step up and make a difference,
secure in Your love and Your power and Your strength.
God, we thank You for the times You enabled us today
and we thank You for the promise now of rest.   AMEN

Scripture Readings

Esther 4:14–17   *Esther is asked to step up for her people*

Mark 1:1–11   *John the Baptist, Preparer of the Way*

Blessing

May you be blessed with insight.

May you be blessed with courage.

May you be blessed with the power to make a difference.

In the Name of God who inspires all prophecy.   Amen

PRAYER NOTES

Dispersed

As you go, proclaim the good news,
'The kingdom of heaven has come near.'

~ Matthew 10:7 ~

Meditation

You breathe out
and we are scattered,
to the very ends of the earth.
Like children blowing dandelions,
we are caught up in the wonder.

We do not journey on a whim,
but rather we float in the hope of sowing something new,
that each and every one of us will imprint something
upon the land that we travel,
and the people that we meet.

Even if we shake the dust off our feet,
we still disturb the ground,
perhaps making it ready for the next breath,
the next ones who are sent:
carriers of hope.
Pray for them,
that they might be welcomed.

Morning Prayer

We can't all go to the far flung corners,
though where we are called to go can seem so distant.
Sometimes, even crossing the road appears too far.
Perhaps, Lord, we need Your sense of perspective,
if we are to carry all that You ask
to the places and people that are waiting for us.
Let Your breath carry us,
Your hope inspire us,
Your love fill us,
and Your gospel remind us,
that it is Your Kingdom we are building.   AMEN

Evening Prayer

When I was under the tree,
You were also there.
When I was in the belly of the whale,
You were also there

Always

You are always there.
You went before me, prepared the way,
yet still I was afraid.
Forgive me, Lord, for the times I did not speak out.
Forgive me, Lord, for the times I did not look or listen.
Forgive me, Lord, for the times I ran the opposite way.
Forgive me, Lord, for the times I tried to hide from You.
Lord, help me
to go where Your wind would blow me.
Lord, help me
to speak the words You give me.
Lord, help me,
every step of the way.   AMEN

Scripture Readings

Matthew 10:5–15   *As you go, proclaim the good news*

Jonah 1:1–3   *Go at once to Nineveh*

Blessing

Bless our coming and going.
Bless our sending and receiving.
Bless our opening and closing.   AMEN

Persecuted

We are afflicted in every way, but not crushed;
perplexed, but not driven to despair;
persecuted, but not forsaken;
struck down but not destroyed.

~ 2 Corinthians 4:8–9 ~

Meditation

'*I am sending you out*
like sheep into the midst of wolves',
You said.
And those first disciples
talked the talk of Gospel
and walked the walk of sacrifice
for Your name's sake.

Like You,
they were hated and humiliated,
badgered and beaten,
interrogated and imprisoned.
Did they really never feel abandoned
or despairing?
Did they never feel confused
about the purpose of all that suffering?
Not even when the end in sight
was to be struck down
for Your name's sake?

I am sorry, Lord,
if I am too easily crushed;
if I prefer an easier way of life
than those of Your persecuted community.
Help me to talk the talk
and walk the walk
even in the face of opposition
for Your name's sake.

Morning Prayer

I give You thanks, Lord,
for the strength, companionship

and love that I receive
from the community with whom I keep the faith.
I give You thanks for the inspiration
of those who have been persecuted
for speaking out and living out
the true beliefs and values of their faith.

Bless all faith communities
in their worship and learning together
and in their mission for justice and peace.
Bless the communities who will today
be persecuted for Your name's sake.   AMEN

Evening Prayer

'Blessed are those who are persecuted
for righteousness' sake,
for theirs is the Kingdom of Heaven.'
You said.
And I trust that includes
those who are persecuted
for their race or religion,
or for their gender or sexuality,
or for their different appearance,
or for their learning difficulties,
or for their illness;

those who are persecuted
for trying to flee danger,
or for wanting a better life for their family,
or for living in the wrong place
or for being a pacifist;
and those who are persecuted
because they are vulnerable
or weak or frail.

Bless them all, Lord –
for You know who they are.
May they trust in the One
who says,
'It is to such as these
that the Kingdom of Heaven belongs.'   AMEN

Scripture Readings

Matthew 10:16–24   *Jesus forewarns the disciples about persecution*

2 Corinthians 4:5–12   *St Paul talks about the persecuted community*

Blessing

May the Holy Parent keep you safe, precious child.
May Christ keep you company, dear sister or brother.
May the Spirit keep you true to your identity and purpose.
And may you rest in God's love now and forevermore.
AMEN

PRAYER NOTES

Ritual

Then I heard the voice of the Lord saying,
'Whom shall I send, and who will go for us?'
And I said, 'Here am I; send me!'

~ Isaiah 6:8 ~

Meditation

There is comfort in the familiar,
in those actions that we repeat
time and again without too much effort on our part.
Rituals that are sacred,
that have a meaning all of their own;
rituals we can perform in our sleep,
yet still have the power –
every once in a while –
to confront us
with the awe and mystery
of a Divine Being:
the One who reaches out of and beyond ritual
to impact our daily grind
with wonder and joy
or challenge and turmoil
or maybe all of these at once;
to reunite us with the God
at the heart of all our ritual,
yet unconfined
by the restraints that we apply.

Morning Prayer

Living God, as we go through the motions,
as we perform our daily rituals
by which we invoke Your name
and Your power,
surprise us with Your presence,
confront us with Your exuberance,
confound us by Your playfulness,
until our actions are once again
infused with meaning
and filled with purpose,

until we reclaim the ability
to expect the unexpected
as we worship
at all the altars of life;
and may the comfort
in familiar rituals
always leave space
for You, our unpredictable God.   AMEN

Evening Prayer

God, we confess that we weren't ready for You today.
We did not expect You to show up
when we invoked Your name in worship;
and, if we're completely honest,
we didn't really want You to barge in
and mess with the order we expected.
But we thank You
that You refused to be confined to those bounds
within which we placed You.
We thank you that You broke free
and surprised us with wonder and joy
and challenged us to hope.
God, do you think You might do
more of the same tomorrow?
and we'll be ready.   AMEN

Scripture Readings

Isaiah 6:6–8   *Isaiah's vision*
Acts 2:1–4   *Gift of the Spirit*

Blessing

The God of ritual and order comfort you;
the Spirit of playful endeavour enthral you;
the blessing of a wholly unpredictable God
confront you in ways beyond your wildest imagining
blessing your life with peace and joy.   AMEN

Rites of Passage

This is my body, which is given for you,
Do this in remembrance of me.

~ Luke 22:19b ~

Meditation

Sacraments and ceremonies
mark the milestones
of our journey with Jesus:
Each rite of passage
signifying a transition,
another stage along the way.

Birth and birthday,
blessing and baptism,
confirmation and confession,
marriage and meal,
anniversary and anointing,
funeral and farewell –
like glimpses through gossamer
these are moments
when promises of God peep through.

Water, grace, Spirit,
oil, wine, bread:
these are the elements
of our rituals.

In sacraments and ceremonies,
we celebrate life,
mourn death,
rejoice in resurrection
and are ourselves transformed
into the practice of God on earth.

Morning Prayer

In the next 24 hours
how many will be born
and how many will die?
How many will marry

and how many will end relationships?
How many will eat in table fellowship
and how many will hunger and thirst?
How many will find God's love
and how many will lose faith?
Bless all Lord,
for whom today
will be a rite of passage.
May Your Spirit guide them
in the journey ahead.   AMEN

Evening Prayer

Your baptism – a transitional moment
for the ones who watched
and saw the dove
and heard the voice:
'This is my Son the beloved
in whom I am well pleased.'
In every baptism now
we imagine that dove coming
down on the water
and hear Your voice
proclaiming every child
to be Your son or daughter.

Baptism is a rite of passage
for the whole community
as the Spirit confirms our belonging.

Your last supper – a transitional moment
for the ones who ate with You
and saw the bread and wine
and heard the voice:
'This is my body broken for you
This is my blood shed for you.'
And in every communion we see
that broken bread and poured-out wine
and hear the words
'For you ....'

Communion is a rite of passage
for the community of the broken
as finding its wholeness in You, Christ,
we are transformed into Your body.   AMEN

Scripture Readings

Matthew 26:26–30	*The last supper*
Acts 16:11–16	*Baptism of Lydia and her household*

Blessing

May God anoint you with His eternal blessing;
may Christ meet you in daily bread and wine
and may the Spirit's baptism fill You with love.   AMEN

PRAYER NOTES

Random

> *In your book were written all the days*
> *that were formed for me,*
> *when none of them as yet existed.*
>
> ~ Psalm 139:16 ~

Meditation

Random happens.
It happens to people who go to church
and it happens to people who don't.
No one escapes random. It's a given.

Cancer happens.
No age, no background, no careful living
gives immunity.
Accidents happen.
The wrong place, the wrong time
and a split second makes the difference.
Encounters happen.
A chance meeting
and at least one life is changed.
Conception and safe birth happen.
Or they don't.
And science cannot answer the soul.

In Your book God
were written all the days
that were formed for each one of us
when none of them as yet existed.
So if it's all preordained
then why can life seem so random?

Morning Prayer

With humility I dare to ask this, Lord,
but if I were You,
would I know already
what is going to happen
in my life, today?
Or, even more importantly,

would I know what's going to happen
to all the people I love?

Sorry to ask, but
I find random quite hard to deal with.
I mean, was there random in Your life, Jesus?
The first twelve and all the other followers,
did You seek them out
or were they just in the right place
at the right time?
And the hundreds needing healed,
how did You pick the few we read of?
Dear Lord,
help me to cope
with the random of today.   AMEN

Evening Prayer

You are Love
and all who live in love
live in You
and You live in them.
Love is not random.
Love is intentional.
We are Love's incarnation.

You are Grace
and all who turn to You
and seek forgiveness
will be healed in spirit.
Grace is not random.
Grace is specific.
Grace from the Cross is a given.

You are Comforter,
the One who guides, tends,
challenges, gifts, transforms
and gathers us.
Comfort is not random.
Comfort is particular.
We are a community of the Comforter.

You are God,
Parent, Son and Holy Spirit

and we are Your children.
Help us to deal with the random
through the mutual love, grace and comfort
that You bestow.   AMEN

Scripture Readings

Psalm 139   *The inescapable God*
John 14:15–31   *The promise of the Holy Spirit*

Blessing

May the God who delights in you,
the Christ who walks with you
and the Spirit who lives in you
hold you in love and bring you safely home.   AMEN

PRAYER NOTES

Companionship

Now when they saw the boldness of Peter and John and realised
that they were uneducated and ordinary men,
they were amazed and recognised them as companions of Jesus.

~ Acts 4:13 ~

Meditation

'They recognised them
as companions of Jesus.'
Imagine being a companion of Jesus,
being with Him
day after day,
from morning till night,
as one of the company of His friends.

Imagine watching Him
at sunrise
as He finds a place apart,
to be alone
in the company of the One
who sent Him.

Imagine walking with Him
along the lanes of Galilee,
now following behind,
now in step with Him,
now right beside Him
as He speaks to you,
only you,
or He listens,
fully focused
on you.

Imagine sitting down with Him,
at nightfall,
all of you, that company of friends,
to eat with Him a simple meal –
that meal at which
He breaks the bread

and pours the wine,
and welcomes all to take and eat and drink.

Morning Prayer

Thank you, Lord,
as I open my eyes this morning,
that I can know
the presence of Christ Jesus
by my side.

I may be alone, or even lonely;
my friends and family may be far away,
but He is close.

When I forget,
or shut Him out,
forgive me, Lord,
and help me today
to be recognised as
one of Jesus' companions.
In His name I pray.   AMEN

Evening Prayer

Lord God,
I know that sometimes,
people are left to sit alone for days,
with no-one to call 'companion'.
I know that sometimes,
families break up
and lifelong companions turn from one another.
I know that sometimes
older people pass away,
and no-one notices for days.

Lord God,
It breaks my heart.

I lift up to You those who are lonely,
but long to laugh with others,
those who desire
togetherness and companionship.

May they find it and be comforted.
And may they know the warmth
of Your presence – wherever they are.
In Jesus name I pray.   AMEN

Scripture Readings

Acts 4	*Known as companions of Jesus*
Romans 16	*Paul sends greetings to his companions*

Blessing

May you live all your days
in the joy of companionship,
and may you know the blessing
of God's presence around you,
now and for ever.   AMEN

PRAYER NOTES

Common Memory

These things I remember, as I pour out my soul:
how I went with the throng, and led them in procession
to the house of God, with glad shouts and songs of thanksgiving,
a multitude keeping festival.

~ Psalm 42:4 ~

Meditation

How we laughed
as we remembered,
the way we had lived
in the old days:
the clothes we wore,
the shoes,
the hair.
How we laughed!

We had changed.
Life had become
so much more serious;
responsibilities
had crowded in;
sadness and loss
had become part of our
experience.

Something had happened
on the way to today
that made us different,
strangers to each other –
and to ourselves.
We had grown up.

How we cried
as we remembered,
how life had changed
over time:
the people
who are no longer here,

the opportunities lost,
the moments wasted.

And our tears
took away the strangeness.
We remembered we were friends,
and we held each other
in a warm embrace,
and we allowed ourselves
to be like children.

Morning Prayer

Holy One,
You have blessed human beings with memory,
a way of keeping treasures in the mind,
a way of learning from experience,
but also a challenge to live with memories of loss.
Every morning, as we open our eyes,
we remember the day before,
the things we need to do today,
and the things we look forward to.
But we remember also the things we dread.
We thank You, God,
that we are not alone with our memories,
but that we share our past with others.
We thank You that, in the sharing,
we can draw closer together.
Help us today, Lord, to use our shared experiences
to strengthen us in our common humanity,
so that in this way we may grow to be one.
In Jesus' name.   AMEN

Evening Prayer

Lord God,
again, today, life has thrown up
so many challenges that had to be faced,
either as individuals, or with those around us.
As we settle down to rest,
there might be memories that disturb our sleep.
We might struggle with things we remember,

things we wish had been different.
Bless us with dreaming, Lord,
Your gift of clearing the mind.
Calm us, and give us respite
from the worries of the day,
so that, on our waking,
we will be refreshed and strengthened
to live through the new day
with courage.
In Jesus' name we pray.   AMEN

Scripture Readings

Ezra 6	*The people remember with joy*
Psalms 42 and 43	*The King remembers with tears*

Blessing

May you remember
the joy of the presence of God
as you live your life
in His way.   AMEN

THE WAY BEYOND

*The journey into the unknown,
beyond the present
and life beyond death.*

*For now we see in a mirror dimly,
but then we will see face to face.
Now I know only in part;
then I will know fully,
even as I have been fully known.
And now faith, hope and love abide;
and the greatest of these is love.*

~ 1 Corinthians 13:12–13 ~

Beyond the Pale

The woman said to him,
'Sir, give me this water, so that I may never be thirsty'

~ John 4:15 ~

Meditation

I thirst.

I am empty and spent.
Despised,
I trudge through
the slurry heat of the mid-day
in search of water.

Without it, I die –
just like those who have loved me.

Straining through the punishing swelter
I wonder if I will make it.

I clutch my water jar
for fear he might smash it.

I see from his outline
that he is not one of ours
nor I one of his.
For I am a woman of Samaria

and yet, he sees me
Sees, **me**
beyond who I am
beyond all the hatred
beyond the disparaging expectation
of the dirty animal his lot, see in me.

But he is so different.
He reaches out to me
beyond the pale
and I begin to see him too
as my salvation.

I no longer thirst
for Christ has found me
beyond the pale.

Morning Prayer

Reaching beyond the pale isn't always easy.
Sometimes it is uncomfortable, sometimes it is costly
but it is the way of the Kingdom,
so Lord help me to do Your will.
Help me to offer something
of Your life-giving quality to others.   AMEN

Evening Prayer

God of the shadows
may we pray for those who still thirst
for those who are still victims of prejudice
and those who are despised by others.
May they find Your love in others
and may Your Kingdom come.   AMEN

Scripture Readings

Philippians 3:7–10	*Losing and finding*
Isaiah 33:15–16	*The assurance of water for those who are righteous*

Blessing

May the outrageous, beyond-the-pale blessing of God
be upon you.
May the unconditional, always-forgiving love of Christ
be with you.
May the incredible, imaginative
and creative blessing of the Spirit
be with you
where you are, and far beyond.   AMEN

Now and Not Yet

No one will say, 'Look, here it is!' or, 'There it is!';
because the Kingdom of God is within you.

~ Luke 17:20 ~

Meditation

The novelist closes her manuscript,
uncorks a celebratory Prosecco.
It is finished!

479 pages, three years' work,
not including countless sheets
balled up and buried
in the recycling bin.

Now, it is finished!
Now and not yet.

She permits herself
this moment of euphoria
before the email arrives
stuffed with edits, scored
with suggestions in red,
requests for clarity in blue
and typos in bright pink.

She will take this rainbow
and begin once again
to reshape the book
until it feels complete enough
to uncork another bottle.

She will celebrate the nows
even when eventually
they become not yets;
moments when the end
drifts into view and, before
the mist draws down,
everything within her
stands and applauds.

Morning Prayer

I embrace the world,
the finished article
and yet unfinished;
creation, recreating.
I embrace traffic horns,
rain on the moors,
shouts of delight,
the scold, the rage,
jumbled stories
freshly articulate,
freedom songs
awaiting voice.
When I hold
the Earth in love,
may I glimpse the heart
of Your Kingdom.   AMEN

Evening Prayer

Another day gone.
Another day less to endure
the wind You send
over the withering grass
and fading flowers.
Another day gone,
spoken for, Your message
to us, Your Word carried
in the wind, a Word
that lasts forever.
Give us ears to hear
and eyes to see beyond
the fleeting present.
Help us to trust in
the Now and Not Yet
You breathe within us.   AMEN

Scripture Readings

| Isaiah 40:6–11 | *All people are like grass* |
| Luke 17:20–21 | *The Kingdom within* |

Blessing

With the same words You will use
when we see You face to face,
may Your blessing fall upon us
as through a dark glass.   AMEN

PRAYER NOTES

Beyond the Horizon

He has described a circle on the face of the waters,
at the boundary between light and darkness.

~ Job 26:10 ~

Meditation

That apparent line that seems to separate
earth from sky,
and perception from insight.
Beyond which,
all that is visible
vanishes to the human eye
and comprehension
becomes like rainbow's end.

Beyond the horizon
lies that far-flung realm of fantasy
where the possibility of possibilities exists
and anything and everything is possible:
the workshop of God
where dreams are birthed
and shaped into reality.

The gap between here and there is often close,
tissue-paper thin,
where visions seep through
and dreams escape.

Once Jesus was asked by the Pharisees
when the Kingdom of God was coming,
and he answered,
'The Kingdom of God is not coming
with things that can be observed;
nor will they say, "Look, here it is!" or "There it is!"
for, in fact, the Kingdom of God is among you'.

Morning Prayer

Lift me up, O God,
so that I may see further,

beyond the horizon of my own limitations
and into the realm of Your Kingdom.

Help me to see
the opportunities that You see,
the beauty of the world as You know it
and the potential of everyone as You do.   AMEN

Evening Prayer

I thank You, God,
that You do not live
in some distant place
beyond the horizon,
but that You mould and fold
the laws of physics
to enter into my space
and beckon me to step towards Yours.
Guide my fragile steps
as I tread towards holiness
in faith, hope, and love.   AMEN

Scripture Readings

> Job 26:1–14   *God at work in Creation*
> Luke 17:20–21   *The Kingdom of God is among you*

Blessing

> May God unfold to you
> the richness of this day
> and bless the potential
> of every moment in it.   AMEN

Otherness of God

'I am God, and there is no other;
I am God, and there is no other like me.'

~ Isaiah 46:9 ~

Meditation

You are unknowable.
You are indescribable.
You are outside our greatest minds
and above our farthest reach.

Your ways are unfathomable
and You are lifted high on Your throne,
in power beyond all measure,
and in love everlasting.

For You alone are God,
and there is no other like You.

Yet You became a man we could know.
You lived a life we could describe.
You taught those who would listen –
that the Kingdom of Heaven
had reached down
and was now close at hand.

You took the way unfathomable
and were lifted high on Your cross,
in power beyond all measure,
and in love everlasting.

For You are God, alone
and there is no other
like You.

Morning Prayer

Almighty God,
with a legion of angels in heaven,
we declare this day:

'Worthy is the Lamb, who was slain
to receive power and wealth
and wisdom and might
and honour and glory and blessing;
and to the one seated on the throne
and to the Lamb
be blessing and honour and glory and might
for ever and ever.'

And so, as I declare his dying and rising,
may I also declare his living
and loving.

And as I set my heart
to the praise of Christ in heaven,
may I always set my hands
to the service of Christ in the world.   AMEN

Evening Prayer

Lord God,
I lay before You the questions I have
about You:
the actions I cannot explain,
the inaction I cannot defend,
the things I don't understand,
and find it difficult to ask You about.

Lord,
let the life of Jesus teach me
all I need to know,
about You.

Lord God,
I lay before You the questions I have
about me:
the actions I cannot explain,
the inaction I cannot defend,
the things I don't understand,
and find it difficult to ask You about.

Lord,
let the life of Jesus teach me

all I need to know,
about me.   AMEN

Scripture Readings

Psalm 139:7–12   *Even the darkness is not dark to you*
Isaiah 6:1–5   *A vision of God in the temple*

Blessing

I bind this day to me forever,
by power of faith, Christ's Incarnation;
his baptism in Jordan river;
his death on cross for my salvation;
his bursting from the spicèd tomb;
his riding up the heavenly way;
his coming at the day of doom:
I bind unto myself today.   AMEN

~ St Patrick ~

PRAYER NOTES

Over the Edge

In truth I have no help in me, and any resource is driven from me.

~ Job 6:13 ~

Meditation

This is where I am:
beyond the outskirts of hope;
outside the edge of despair;
way past the point of caring –
I saw that marker in my rearview mirror
a long way back.

So, leave me here,
and leave me be.
Do not try to tell me that You understand.
Do not try to wipe away my tears
or soothe me with words of comfort.
For this is where I need to be –
in the realness of my pain
and the darkness of my world.

Just be patient
and wait for me –
until I return
in my own time.
For that is when I will need You.

Morning Prayer

Lord Jesus Christ,
You knew the pain and anguish of suffering.
You wept.
You felt the sting of betrayal.
You suffered the long dark night of the soul.

My pain is real.
It claws at my soul,
it cuts my spirit,
and nothing can be said to take it away.
So, save me from the false platitudes

and well-meaning kindness of those
who seek to rescue me.

Just be by my side –
ready for when I need You.   AMEN

Evening Prayer

As the shadows lengthen on another day
and the night creeps in,
may sleep ease my worries
and refresh my tired and weary soul.

Help me, O God,
to see the promise of a new sunrise.
Strengthen me to face the challenges of tomorrow
and leave behind the baggage of today.

And when I awake,
remind me that You still love me.   AMEN

Scripture Readings

Job 6:1–13   *The Lament of Job*
Psalm 88   *A Psalm of Lament*

Blessing

May there someday be … hope.
May there someday be … happiness.
May there someday be … peace.   AMEN

Letting Go

If they had been thinking of the land they had left behind they would have had the opportunity to return

~ Hebrews 11:15 ~

Meditation

Letting go isn't easy
but the alternative is death.

It's always been home to me
a familiar skyline
well-known faces.
The smell of cooking.
The hubbub of friends
living their lives;
barely worth a passing thought until it is gone

until the skyline
lies in rubble and smoke.
The familiar destroyed
the sirens announce another fire, another rape,
another murder.

With my sons in one arm
and the charred belongings of my love in another.
They have taken her from us.
They have taken everything we called home.

My life,
not always easy, yet full of the ordinary,
is now dead.

It is time to let go.
I cannot think of home.
I must find another
for the sake of my boys
for the memory of my love

I am letting go
of one living hell
for another.

Hoping to God, that there will be a new day
worth living for

Morning Prayer

Forgive me God for not appreciating life itself,
for taking my work, family and friends for granted.
Let me have the courage to truly see what I have
and what I no longer need.
May I let go of the prejudices and fears
of a comfortable life
and see You in all those I meet.

Evening Prayer

God of the night
we pray for safety
for the men, women and children
who travel this world in search of freedom.
May You touch the plight of the refugee,
and may we reach out with welcoming love.   Amen

Scripture Readings

Hebrews 11	*Thinking of the land they had left behind*
Matthew 25:31–46	*Ministering to Christ in the stranger*

Blessing

As we go in peace
may others do so too.
May Your blessing be upon us
and all those who seek Your promised land.
Amen

Dying

When David's time to die drew near,
he charged his son, Solomon saying,
'I am about to go the way of all the earth.
Be strong, be courageous.'

~ 1 Kings 2:1–2 ~

Meditation

I am about to go
the way of all the earth.
One of the two certainties of life,
death is the great equaliser.
No point in worrying about the event.
But, O dear Lord,
my soul trembles
when I think of dying.
How will it be?
It is not the same way for everyone.

Will it be a long, hard journey
that gives us all time to prepare,
ends neatly tied up,
fond farewells
and final words I will not hear –
'*It was a blessing*'?

Or will there be a short cut,
no time to think or plan, just
'*Life's been great, goodbye!*'
leaving loved ones devastated?

Whatever way it is to be, Lord,
when I have gone beyond the point
where anyone here can accompany me –
may I know Your presence
in the grace of forgiveness
and hear the beginning words,
'*I am the resurrection and the life*'.
And may I find that You are leading me
along the Garden path.

Morning Prayer

God of life and death,
may I die prepared.
From this day onwards
help me to unpack for the journey.
Let me give away all that
I cannot take with me.
May I be left with only what I need
to live a hospitable life.

But what I can take with me,
are the people I love
because You have promised
there will be reunion
in Christ.
So, inspire me to say the words
and do the things
I would want to
if I thought I was going to die tonight.
'I love you' is always such a good start.   Amen

Evening Prayer

Bless all, dear Lord,
who are in the late evening of their lives.
May those who know it not fear the night
but find meaning in the dawn of each new day.
And for the ones who are unaware
of tomorrow's journey,
may they be delivered safely.

Someone once wrote,
'Death is nothing at all'.
Really?
Personally or vicariously
we experience dying
and everyone experiences loss
but we cannot touch death.
It is sacred. It is holy.
And death is everything.
For only death leads us

to the dawn of eternal life.
Bless me and all whom I love.
Bless all who will die tonight.   AMEN

Scripture Readings

1 Kings 2:1–9	*David's final instruction to Solomon*
John 14:1–4	*Jesus promises to prepare a place for us*

Blessing

Go with joy my friends.
Go with love my family.
Go with grace my neighbours.
Go with peace my community.
And until we meet again
may peace, love, compassion and grace
fill you and the life of the world.   AMEN

PRAYER NOTES

Resurrection

O God, you are my God, I seek you, my soul thirsts for you;
my flesh faints for you, as in a dry and weary land where there is
no water.

~ Psalm 63:1 ~

Meditation

I know this life,
as well as I'll ever know anything.
I know its high mountain tops
and its deep, dark, shadowy valleys.
I wait for its surprises
and expect its challenges.
I know there are days filled with fear,
and others that overflow with joy.
I know, too, the worry,
the sadness, the despair,
that living this life can bring.
And yet, I love this life;
moment by moment I cherish it,
and I never want it to end.

But the day will come
when I will take my last breath
and I'll be gone.

Gone where?
Gone anywhere?

Resurrection?
I don't know resurrection life.

But I place my trust in the One who said,
'I am the resurrection and the life ...'
And so I know that
resurrection is to live again,
a new life,
life in all its fullness,
life in the very presence of God,
the Giver of life,

the One who knows me
better than I know myself.

How could I ask for more?

Morning Prayer

I'm glad to be alive, Lord.
I'm glad to see again this morning
the beauty of the earth, our blue planet.
I'm looking forward again to spending time
with the people I will meet today.
Thank You, God, for every breath You give me.

Help me to savour the moments of this day
as I go about the business of living my life.
I praise You for it,
in Jesus' name.   AMEN

Evening Prayer

Another day has passed, Lord God,
and my life goes on.
But for many around the earth
this has been their last day.
I didn't know them,
but You remember them Lord, in all their diversity:
people of all ages, some not yet born;
people from every country and of every culture
have come to the end of their lives.
So many in these troubled times
have died through the violence of others.
Lord, I pray for all their loved ones in their sadness
that they may have hope,
the hope that this life is truly not all there is,
and that after the darkness of death
comes the light of the resurrection.
In the name of Jesus I pray.   AMEN

Scripture Readings

Psalm 63   *Longing for life in God's presence*
1 Corinthians 15   *Resurrection life*

Blessing

May you know the deep blessing
of living this life in the sure and certain hope
of the resurrection to eternal life
through Jesus Christ
who is the resurrection and the life.   AMEN

PRAYER NOTES

Heaven

Then I saw a new heaven and a new earth.

~ Revelation 21:1 ~

Meditation

Unimaginable heaven –
full of trumpets, thrones,
great jewels, a street of glass
and within a stone's throw
the place of condemnation.
That kind of heaven
does nothing for me.

No more heaven.
No more tears, no more death,
no more mourning, no more crying
no more pain,
no more thirst!
Now, that kind of heaven
does something for me.

For always heaven –
always in God's presence,
always reunited with those we love
always peace, always community,
always perfect communion.
That is the kind of heaven
I long for.

Morning Prayer

Today, Lord,
inspire my image of heaven;
reveal to me
that part of heaven
that I need to believe in.

Then, help me, I pray,
to live out my image of heaven,
in every thought, word and deed.

May I live as though heaven
is present on earth.

Be with me, God,
clothe me with grace
and lead me safely to complete revelation.   AMEN

Evening Prayer

Whatever image of heaven
is given to each of us
I believe heaven is a place
where all time becomes love.
Thank You for all the times today
when I gave and when I received love.
Redeem the times I did not.

Please bless all I love –
the ones here and the ones
forever in Your company.

Please bless also all who so need
to believe in heaven,
in reunion
in Your holding safe of memories
and in Your restoration of all creation.

And please, Lord,
may those in the valley
of tears, death, mourning,
crying, pain or thirst
be comforted
and uplifted on angel's wings.   AMEN

Scripture Readings

Matthew 22:1–14   *Parable of the wedding banquet*
Revelation 21:1–7   *A new heaven and a new earth*

Blessing

Finish then Thy new creation:
pure and spotless let us be;
let us see Thy great salvation

perfectly restored in Thee,
changed from glory into glory,
till in heaven we take our place,
till we cast our crowns before Thee
lost in wonder, love, and praise.   AMEN

~ Charles Wesley ~

PRAYER NOTES

Revelation

May the God of Peace sanctify you entirely
~ 1 Thessalonians 5:23 ~

Meditation

I don't do sitting still.
I don't stop.
The idea of taking my time is anathema.

I used to race through halls of mirrors and mazes
desperate to get to the end,
be the winner
and move on to the next attraction.

Imagine my confusion
when I found the labyrinth

I stepped on.
The first few steps, and turns
quick – just like always.

But then, I slowed;
I stepped back, retraced,
reflected and dared to pray

I realised then
there's no secret exit –
no dead ends,

just a slow, steady circle of eternity.

And I see it.
No,
I feel it.
God, full circle,
enveloping me.

I am whole.

Morning Prayer

Gracious God, in the harried, hurriedness of the day
give me the courage to be still.

Allow me to pause and reflect.
For I know I move too quickly
and I miss You in the minutiae of the moment.
Let's not let that happen today.   AMEN

Evening Prayer

Has today been hurried?
Did I stop?
Did I do all that I prayed for this morning?
In this moment of prayer,
help me to cast my mind's eye over the day.
Let me see Your face in the people I met.
Let me hear Your cry in the people I walked past.
Let me be still, just for a moment.
And maybe, one day, I will get it
and actually be still
in Your presence.   AMEN

Scripture Readings

1 Thessalonians 5   *Peace and salvation*
Revelation 21   *A new heaven and a new earth*

Blessing

Deep peace of the running wave to you.
Deep peace of the flowing air to you.
Deep peace of the quiet earth to you.
Deep peace of the shining stars to you.
Deep peace of the gentle night to you.
Moon and stars pour their healing light on you.
Deep peace of Christ,
of Christ the light of the world to you.
Deep peace of Christ to you.   AMEN

~ Ancient Celtic blessing ~

PRAYER ACTIVITIES

Seeking Refuge

While every refugee's story is different
and their anguish personal, they all share
a common thread of uncommon courage –
the courage not only to survive,
but to persevere and rebuild their shattered lives.

~ Antonio Guterres ~
Former Portuguese Prime Minister and
U.N. High Commissioner for Refugees 2005–2015

There is a global refugee crisis. People flee countries that are at war with another nation or suffering a civil war. These people need refuge. We recognise them as victims. They provoke our compassion and our desire to help in any way we can.

In what ways are you helping or can you help, either as an individual or as part of a faith or local community group?

Find out what third-sector organisations/charities in your local area are supporting refugees arriving in your own neighbourhood, city or country.

Explore what you can do to support refugees held in makeshift refugee camps across the world – try websites for charities such as Tearfund, Save the Children, Christian Aid, Oxfam, Spirit Aid, Red Cross – there may be also a few local charities that are contributing to international relief programmes.

Pray for the work of the charities you have identified or researched.

Pray for the refuge, safe transport, welcome, rehoming, clothing, education, health care, employment and befriending of every refugee.

Pray that each refugee is able to persevere and to rebuild their shattered lives – from the youngest to the oldest. (It might help to download or cut out images of actual individuals or families who are refugees as a focus.)

Read out loud the quotation for this prayer activity.

How often do you view refugees as heroes, or do you see only the victim?

To what extent do you recognise and draw inspiration from these ordinary people who have shown such extra-ordinary courage?

Many men leave their wives and children behind in a dangerous situation while they make a dangerous journey to seek refuge. When they have found it then they have to find the means to bring their family to the safe place.

Take one of your pictures of a refugee family. Make an award for bravery and attach it to the picture.

What can refugees teach you in your faith and in your lifestyle? Reflect on this.

Meditate on the verse

> *'Be merciful to me, O God,*
> *be merciful to me,*
> *for in you my soul takes refuge;*
> *in the shadow of your wings I will take refuge,*
> *until the destroying storms pass by.'*

~ Psalm 57:1 ~

When have you needed refuge from 'destroying storms'?

Where did you find it?

Give thanks.

PRAYER NOTES

PRAYER NOTES

Being Tested

One small crack does not mean you are broken,
It means that you were put to the test
And didn't fall apart.

~ Linda Poindexter ~

The story goes that in fifteenth-century Japan, a Shogun sent a damaged pot to China to be repaired. When it was returned, held together with staples, the Shogun decided to take on the repair himself. Mixing gold dust into the adhesive resin that would hold the broken pieces together meant that what was once seen as imperfect could become something greater than the sum of its parts.

The Japanese art of Kintsugi was born.

Translated as 'Golden Joinery', there is no attempt to hide or mask the damage, but the repair is illuminated and becomes integral to the form, making it in a sense a work of art.

Some people would say that it is through testing and trial that we discover who we really are. That character perhaps cannot be developed in the comfortable or quiet times, but rather that in the experience of trial our soul is strengthened, our vision cleared and our creativity birthed.

Kintsugi honours both the cracks and the repair, allowing both to speak and a new story to emerge.

Perhaps, in your worshipping communities, you could explore your stories of God's 'golden joinery' in your lives through the creating of a mosaic. Mosaics are pieces of art that create a picture (perhaps even tell a story) out of broken pieces of pottery or tiles.

The songwriter Michael Card says of creativity:

Creativity does not truly come from the popularised image of the tormented artist, struggling with the muse.

True creativity is born in community as men and women of God listen to each other (and to Him); as we seek to understand each other's woundedness and strengths ...

As you build your mosaic, perhaps you could share stories of testing or trial as you take turns to add to the mosaic.

Working on pieces of art such as a mosaic can give space for reflection.

Maybe this space is helpful to use while reflecting personally on times when you felt tested or were indeed broken by the circumstances in which you found yourself.

We all have the opportunity to view the pieces of our lives – some that are smooth, some with ragged edges, some split and broken.

All come with a story and an opportunity.

Seek God for guidance as you reflect on your own stories.

PRAYER NOTES

PRAYER NOTES

Sacrificing

The ultimate test of man's conscience may be his willingness to sacrifice everything today for future generations whose words of thanks will not be heard.

~ Gaylord Nelson ~

Gaylord Nelson was a pioneer in understanding the damage we were doing to the earth and in 1970 he began the Earth Day movement working towards a better understanding of energy conservation and our wastefulness.

Think back over your life. How have attitudes in general changed?

Do you recognise times of wastefulness as a society?

What about personally?

Did you resist change initially?

Do you embrace ecological stewardship, or do you abide it?

Our wastefulness can be seen as a wanton sacrificing of the Earth.
Now we are being called to sacrifice some of our habits for the good of the Earth.

Can you do better?
Can you sacrifice some of your car time or air travel?

Observe an Eco-Sabbath: For one day, afternoon or hour a week, don't buy anything; don't use machines; don't switch on anything electrical; don't cook; don't answer your phone and, in general, don't use any resources.

Try the 30-day rule. If you think you want to buy something new, wait thirty days to make sure you really need/want it before you buy.

Simplify: Simplify your life as much as possible.

Only keep belongings that you use/enjoy on a regular basis. By making the effort to reduce what you own, you will naturally purchase less/create less waste in the future.

Determine your impact on the environment by determining your ecological footprint – http://www.footprint network.org/en/index.php/GFN/page/calculators/ – this calculator gives you a great way to determine how you are impacting the environment.

Pray and reflect on how we treat God's Earth.

Should we be proud?

Should we be ashamed?

What can we do?

What can we pray?

It's up to you …

PRAYER NOTES

PRAYER NOTES

Resurrecting

Perhaps [the critics are right and] the drama is played out now, and Jesus is safely dead and buried. Perhaps. It is ironical and entertaining to consider that at least once in the world's history those words might have been said with complete conviction, and that was on the eve of the Resurrection.

~ Dorothy L. Sayers, *The Whimsical Christian: 18 Essays* ~

After death something new begins, over which all powers of the world of death have no more might.

~ Dietrich Bonhoeffer ~

The passing of time brings loss:

we lose precious possessions; jobs; pets; childhood; youth; friendships; family connections; much-loved people.

Some losses may not be for ever. When something we value is lost and then found again, it is a little bit like a resurrection. A treasured piece of jewellery is mislaid, but then turns up again, and we are glad. An old dog dies and we are sad, but one day a new puppy arrives and brings us joy. A job is lost, but another opportunity opens up for us.

Some losses are for ever, but what was lost may be replaced by other things: childhood and youth won't come back, but we may gain wisdom from life experience.

Some losses may need a little work to reverse: friendships and family connections may be restored, or resurrected, through forgiveness and love.

Some losses, however, are for good – without the One who has the power to bring life again, the power of resurrection.

Is there something in your life that once was lost, and now is found? If you can hold it, pick it up now. If it's intangible, bring it to mind. Give thanks to God for finding it again.

Do you miss a friendship you lost through some kind of misunderstanding?

Do you miss the presence in your life of a family member for a similar reason?

You may want to think seriously about ways of making peace with them, and then put your plan into action.

As for the ones you miss because they have died, it may help if you consciously place them into the love and care of the Lord who is the Resurrection and the Life. You may want to do this in writing, in your own hand, and keep the note in an envelope, with a photograph of the person. Whenever you feel the loss, take out the note and read it again.

Let your prayers flow out of your experience of loss and restoration, and the hope of the resurrection in God's time.

PRAYER NOTES

PRAYER NOTES

Living in the Spirit

We often talk about faith when in the strictly Christian sense it is not faith ... It is when all confidence in yourself or in human support, and also in God in an immediate way, is extinct, when every probability is extinct, when it is dark as on a dark night – it is indeed death we are describing – then comes the life-giving Spirit and brings faith. This faith is stronger than the whole world; it has the power of eternity; it is the Spirit's gift from God.

~ Søren Kierkegaard, *For Self-Examination*, 1851 ~

Danish philosopher Søren Kierkegaard had a rather bleak outlook on the reality of faith at times, but that doesn't mean he was wrong. When a positive outcome seems inevitable, it doesn't require much faith to make it happen. We know things will be fine. But when a positive outcome feels uncertain, and we call to God and don't sense any immediate answer, that's when we have the choice either to give up or to trust in the Holy Spirit. The Spirit comes with the gift of faith, the 'power of eternity', even if we are not immediately aware of it.

Try using a psalm as a prayer. You can pick virtually any psalm at random and find something in it, either as a song of protest, praise or confession. Read it slowly and thoughtfully and bring to mind both your own life, the lives of others you know and situations you are concerned about, and read them into the psalm. As an example, Psalm 20 would read like:

1. *The LORD answer you in the day of trouble!*
   The name of the God of Jacob protect you!

and:

7. *Some take pride in chariots, and some in horses,*
   but our pride is in the name of the LORD our God.

Reading the psalms in this way is a turning towards God and away from cynicism and apathy. Pray that this attitude will spill into your life continually throughout the day and that you will be granted the faith that comes from living in the Spirit.

Now, try composing your own short psalm. Be honest with your thoughts and feelings. Don't hold anything back. But close the psalm by invoking the Holy Spirit to bring a depth of faith that will make a real difference to your life.

PRAYER NOTES

PRAYER NOTES

Forgiving

Though with their high wrongs I am struck to th' quick,
Yet with my nobler reason, 'gainst my fury
Do I take part. The rarer action is
In virtue than in vengeance.

~ Prospero, from *The Tempest*
by William Shakespeare, Act 5, scene 1 ~

Prospero isn't a natural forgiver. He wants to get revenge on his enemies for wrongs done in the past (and present!) but, during the course of the play, he begins to realise that reconciliation is a better way. However, that can't happen unless he forgives those people he least wants to forgive. He employs reason against his natural fury and decides on the 'rarer action'.

Think of people you have found it easy to forgive. What made it so easy?

Pray that you might forgive others when it is easy to do so, rather than store up feelings of revenge.

Pray for others you think might find it easy to forgive you if they only made that decision.

Think of people you have managed to forgive, even though you found it hard to do so.

What gave you the strength to forgive?

What obstacles did you have to overcome?

Pray that you might learn from those times when it comes to forgiving and being forgiven now and in the future.

Think of people you have found it impossible to forgive. Sometimes it is extraordinarily difficult, especially when feelings of hurt or betrayal run deep or affect our lives in unpredictable ways, and no one should feel guilt over finding forgiveness hard to offer.

We may know, with Prospero, that 'the rarer action is/ In virtue than in vengeance', but knowing something is often simpler than enacting it.

Ask God to be near you and, in His time, to make the impossible possible again. And 'pray for those who persecute you' (Matthew 5:44), as Jesus tells us.

Think of situations in the world where revenge and hatred are in continuous cycle.

Pray that the Holy Spirit might make forgiveness and reconciliation possible, and that we might be enabled to play whatever part we can, great or small, in bringing about a more peaceful world.

PRAYER NOTES

PRAYER NOTES

Resting

Every now and then go away, have a little rest, for when you come back to your work your judgment will be surer. Go some distance away because then the work appears smaller and more of it can be taken in at a glance and a lack of harmony and proportion is more readily seen.

~ Leonardo Da Vinci (15 April 1452 – 2 May 1519) ~

And on the seventh day God finished the work that he had done, and he rested on the seventh day from all the work that he had done.

~ Genesis 2:2 ~

There can be no doubt that resting is important for the health and wellbeing of human beings. According to the book of Genesis, God the Creator himself rested from His work of creating. Furthermore, provision for a day of rest for all human beings is part of God's Ten Commandments (Deuteronomy 5:14).

And, as Leonardo tells us in the above quotation, rest gives us a new perspective in relation to our work.

Most people lead busy lives filled with work, both in paid employment and outside it.

Those who care for others – perhaps children or other dependants – are especially busy.

Many in our society find it hard to create space for themselves to be at rest.

Of course, rest is difficult to define.
What some people find restful might drive others to distraction.
The key is to find what is restful for you.

In a quiet moment, away from everything that might be intrusive, sit down and make a list of all the things you have done in your life that have helped you rest and relax; then make another list, this time of things you have not yet tried, but you imagine might help you be at rest.

Then choose one activity (or inactivity) from each list and mark a time for it in your diary. Let nothing distract you from your plans (except maybe fire and pestilence) and, when the time comes, give yourself completely to the kind of resting you have chosen. Afterwards, for future reference, in your diary or on your lists, give your time of resting a mark out of ten.

Then repeat the whole process at regular intervals.

You may have someone in your family or in your circle of friends who finds it very difficult to make time for rest. Maybe you can find a way of enabling them to create a breathing space and get away from it all.

In your prayers you may want to remember those who cannot rest, and those whose rest is involuntary; those whose work is all-consuming, and those who look for work and find none; those in developing countries who must work long hours for very little pay, and for whom rest is but a distant dream.

PRAYER NOTES

PRAYER NOTES

Expressing

Walking is easy ...
but it requires faith to find the right path.

~ John Twelve Hawks, *The Traveler* ~

Faith is not just something you have,
it's something you do.

~ Barack Obama, speech, 1 December 2006 ~

We express our faith in a combination of different ways, from where and how we worship to what we say and do in our everyday lives. All of these things have been shaped, and continue to be shaped, by the myriad and variety of influences of people, places and events in our lives.

Create a mind map* that shows your own faith journey – highlighting the people, places and events (both positive and negative) that have helped to shape your beliefs and understanding of God.

Once you have finished your map, use it to identify the main influences on your faith and reflect on the core values/principles behind them.

Consider how you express these values/principles in your life. Do you find it hard to put any of these values/principles into practice?

Pray for these areas of your life and seek ways that might help you to develop the expression of your faith.

You may wish to do this exercise over at least two sessions with breaks between creating, reflecting and responding to your mind map.

You may also find it helpful to deal with one branch/line of your map at a time – considering your response to each section before you return to a different section at a later date.

* If you are unfamiliar with the concept of a mind map try looking for examples online or in your local library before you start your own. Here are some basic guidelines for creating your own mind map:

1. Start your drawing in the centre of the page.

2. Radiate out from the centre of your mind map (much like the branches of a tree).

3. Make each branch follow a particular theme (e.g. family).

4. Use at least three different colours.

5. Use images, symbols, codes or words throughout your mind map.

6. Each word or image is best sitting on its own line/branch.

7. Highlight key words using UPPER CASE or **bold** print.

8. Use emphasis, colours or symbols to show associated points on your mind map.

9. Develop your own style that is meaningful to you.

PRAYER NOTES

PRAYER NOTES

Learning

Education is the kindling of a flame – not the filling of a vessel.

~ Socrates ~

School might have been the best days of your life.

A happy fulfilling experience,
a place filled with memories of playground pals,
a place of encouragement leading to further learning;
or perhaps a time you would rather forget.

Difficult memories lurk in the shadows;
harsh teaching, poor conditions, scarce resources,
bullying or difficulty learning.

Learning has evolved and changed dramatically over the last fifty years. In many ways it is unrecognisable, becoming more collaborative and even fun.

If learning was a joy for you, give thanks for the teachers you cherished.

If it was a tough time, pray and reflect on the reasons.

Let go and forgive if that is what needs to be done.

If you struggled with learning and were later diagnosed in adult life with conditions such as dyslexia, give thanks that early detection and understanding is more commonplace today.

Pray for children who encounter learning difficulties today.

Write your own school report as it should have been written.

Did you pull the wool over the teachers' eyes?

Could you have tried harder?

Did you receive undeserved praise?

Were you misunderstood?

Read your report that you have written. Is it vastly different to what you received at school?

Pray for teachers as they try to encourage the best out of future generations.

Finally, remember places where education is a privilege for a few; pray for women, men and children who have not been to school, where poverty, famine or war has stripped them of the possibility of schooling and generations will suffer for years to come.

Give thanks and pray for charities such as Mary's Meals, which help provide the possibilities of education in the developing world.

PRAYER NOTES

PRAYER NOTES

Harvesting

*Our deep respect for the land and its harvest
is the legacy of generations of farmers
who put food on our tables, preserved our landscape,
and inspired us with a powerful work ethic.*

~ James H. Douglas, Jr. ~
Lawyer and American statesman who died in 1988

In what ways do you show respect for the land and its harvest?

It is 'our way' to say 'grace' before each meal to thank God for creation, for harvest and for all who sowed, grew, reaped, transported, produced, sold to us and, perhaps, made our food.

Give thanks to God for all that makes possible the food that we eat.

Write a grace that you can use with your family, friends, or faith group. A good resource for this is 'Blessed be our table' by Neil Paynter (Wild Goose Publications, ISBN 1 901557 72 3).

Khalil Gibran in his book, 'The Garden of the Prophet' wrote, '*Pity the nation that wears a cloth it does not weave and eats a bread it does not harvest*'.

Does the above quotation challenge you?

Go round a supermarket, and notice the fresh produce and other items that come from abroad.

Notice how many are Fairtrade certified and how many are not.

Pray for those who do not get their fair share of the world's harvest.

What can you do about it as an individual or as part of a group effort?

Explore the Fairtrade website www.fairtrade.org.uk for ideas.

When you reap the harvest of your land, you shall not reap to the very edges of your field, or gather the gleanings after your harvest. You shall not strip your vineyard bare, or gather the fallen grapes of your vineyard. You shall leave them for the poor and the alien: I am the Lord your God.

~ Leviticus 19:9–10 ~

How do you see this law written in Leviticus being enacted today, in your own country?

PRAYER NOTES

PRAYER NOTES

Waiting

Patience is Power.
Patience is not absence of action;
rather it is 'timing'
it waits on the right time to act,
for the right principles
and the right way.

~ Fulton J. Sheen ~

Often we hear people recite the phrase –

Good things come to those who wait.

I didn't agree with this statement until I found that, in the waiting, I became more aware of the value I ascribed to that or whom on which I waited. This was the better part that I was left with, beyond the desire to get exactly what I wanted when I wanted it.

In the waiting there can be space (if we look hard enough). Sometimes it can be hard to find at first, but then as you adjust to what is happening, you can find it.

Space

A new rhythm perhaps,

ebb and flow

like breathing.

Sometimes after exercise we can be almost breathless, having to work hard to regulate our breathing.
At other times, as we start to relax, a deep exhale can say more than a thousand words!

Jesus visited the house of Martha and her sister Mary. While Martha was concerned about tidying and busying herself, Mary sat and listened to the words of Jesus.
When Martha asked Jesus to chastise Mary and to encourage her to join Martha in the busyness, He said – 'Martha, Martha, you are worried and distracted by many things; there is need of only one thing. Mary has chosen the better part, which will not be taken away from her' (Luke 10:38–42).

When we wait, do we consider how we wait?

Are we frantically busy, filling our time with anything to take our mind off the space?

Or, do we wait patiently?

Do we worry about what might happen?

Do we involve God at all?

You can consider these questions in times of personal reflection or if you want to use them in a group, you could have conversations around these questions and the following prompts.

Ask people to share a story of a time they waited and were surprised.

Share a story about a time you waited and were disappointed.

Would you describe yourself as a patient or impatient person?

Share a story of a time when you were still before God.

Finally, you could keep a 'waiting journal', noting what you waited for during the day – emails, buses, trains or that parcel you ordered, and then reflect on how you felt during each of the periods of waiting.

PRAYER NOTES

PRAYER NOTES

Incarnating

Man's maker was made man,
that He, Ruler of the stars,
might nurse at His mother's breast;
that the Bread might hunger,
the Fountain thirst,
the Light sleep,
the Way be tired on its journey;
that the Truth might be accused of false witness,
the Teacher be beaten with whips,
the Foundation be suspended on wood;
that Strength might grow weak;
that the Healer might be wounded;
that Life might die.

~ Augustine of Hippo (*Sermons* 191.1) ~

Oh yes, you shaped me first inside, then out;
you formed me in my mother's womb.
I thank you, High God – you're breathtaking!
Body and soul, I am marvellously made!
I worship in adoration – what a creation!
You know me inside and out,
you know every bone in my body;
You know exactly how I was made, bit by bit,
how I was sculpted from nothing into something.
Like an open book, you watched me grow
from conception to birth;
all the stages of my life
were spread out before you,
The days of my life all prepared
before I'd even lived one day.

~ Psalm 139:13–16 (The Message) ~

UNICEF estimates that an average of 353,000 babies are born each day around the world. Since not all births are registered or recorded the crude birth rate is estimated at an average of 18.9 births per 1,000 population. That equates to 255 births globally per minute or 4.3 births every second (as of December 2013 estimate).

We sometimes assume that the arrival of a new baby will be a time of joy and excitement for future parents, but it can also be a worrying time – especially for those expecting their first child.

Pray for those who are expecting the birth of a child and the worries they may be carrying, for example about their own health; their unborn child's health; finances; and future family life.

Pray for those who struggle with anxiety, fear and/or depression as they seek to adjust to the new set of demands that a baby brings.

Pray for the work of the Bluebell Perinatal Depression Service Scotland (http://www.crossreach.org.uk/bluebell-pnd-service) or for the work of a similar organisation in your own country.

Consider ways in which you might be able to support them in their work.

Pray for those who yearn to be mothers and fathers, but are unable to be so.

Pray for those couples who face the emotionally and physically draining routes of IVF, surrogacy and adoption as they seek to become parents.

PRAYER NOTES

PRAYER NOTES

Acknowledgements

Pray Now 'People of the Way' was prepared by members of the Pray Now Writing Group: Adam Dillon, Peggy Ewart-Roberts, Carol Ford, Mark Foster, Rob A Mackenzie, Liz Crumlish, Graham Fender-Allison and Phill Mellstrom.

Daily headline Scripture quotations are taken from the New Revised Standard Version, © 1989 Division of Christian Education of the National Council of Churches of Christ in the United States of America, published by Oxford University Press.

With special thanks to Robert McQuistan, Phill Mellstrom, Eva Elder and Lynn Hall for their work in preparing the final manuscript.